Fa
Parler

French for beginners

Support Book

Angela Aries and
Dominique Debney

4th edition

HODDER
EDUCATION

AN HACHETTE UK COMPANY

Acknowledgement

The extract from «Knock ou le triomphe de la médecine» by Jules Romains on page 323 and in the recordings is reproduced by permission of Editions Gallimard.

Orders: please contact Bookpoint Ltd, 130 Milton Park, Abingdon, Oxon OX14 4SB. Telephone: (44) 01235 827720. Fax: (44) 01235 400454. Lines are open from 9.00–5.00, Monday to Saturday, with a 24 hour message answering service. You can also order through our website www.hoddereducation.co.uk

If you have any comments to make about this, or any of our other titles, please send them to educationenquiries@hodder.co.uk

British Library Cataloguing in Publication Data
A catalogue record for this title is available from The British Library.

ISBN 978 0 340 94023 5

First Edition Published 1986
Fourth Edition Published 2007
Impression number   10 9 8 7 6 5 4 3
Year   2010 2009
Copyright © 2007 Angela Aries and Dominique Debney

Cover photo from Eitan Simanor/Photographer's Choice/Getty Images
Typeset by Transet Limited, Coventry, England.
Printed in Great Britain by CPI Antony Rowe, Chippenham, Wiltshire

Contents

Contents

Key

Première unité

avez-vous compris? (p.3) **1** vrai, **2** faux (il est guide pendant les vacances), **3** faux (elle habite dans l'ouest de la France, **4** vrai, **5** faux (c'est une ville de Provence), **6** faux (elle travaille dans une usine), **7** faux (Ils habitent à Quimper depuis six mois), **8** vrai, **9** vrai, **10** vrai, **11** vrai, **12** faux (il vend des médicaments).

à vous! (p.4) **1 a Jeanne** habite à Luçon en Vendée dans l'ouest de la France. Elle est professeur de sciences naturelles. Elle est célibataire. **b Annick et Yves** habitent à Quimper en Bretagne depuis six mois. Ils sont fiancés. Annick est fonctionnaire. Elle travaille dans un bureau. Yves travaille en plein air parce qu'il est marin-pêcheur. . **c Claire** est de Normandie. Elle a un appartement à Rouen, 160 avenue de Bretagne. Elle travaille à temps partiel parce qu'elle a deux enfants, un fils de onze ans, Paul, et une fille de sept ans, Élisabeth. **d Guillaume** a 21 ans. Il est étudiant à Paris. Pendant les vacances, pour se faire un peu d'argent, il travaille pour la société Tourama; il sert de guide à des groupes de touristes. **e Henri** est divorcé et il n'a pas d'enfants, mais un chat très affectueux qui s'appelle Moustache. Il a une petite maison à Nuits-Saint-Georges, près de Dijon, en Bourgogne. Il est pharmacien, mais il préfère le bon vin aux médicaments!

f Sylvie est de Grasse, en Provence, dans le sud-est de la France. Elle est ouvrière dans une usine de parfums. Elle n'est pas mariée. Son numéro de téléphone est le 04 93 35 09 12! **2 a** où / à / en / dans, **b** avez / j'ai / qui, **c** ne / pas, **d** travaillez / suis, **e** êtes / de, **f** depuis.

avez-vous compris? (p.11) **Qualités:** beau, toujours de bonne humeur, intelligent, riche, spirituel, courageux, honnête, modeste, douée, jolie, mince, élégante, gentil. **Défauts:** bavarde, curieuse, nul, toujours de mauvaise humeur, gourmande, pas très patient, têtu, paresseux, timide. **1** Antoine et Dominique, **2** François Muller, **3** Annette, **4** Mme Brède, **5** François Muller, **6** Claire Ouate, **7** Antoine et Dominique, **8** François Muller, **9** Claire Ouate, **10** Mme Brède, **11** Simon, **12** Mme Brède, **13** Antoine et Laurent, **14** Chantal, **15** Mme Brède, **16** Claire Ouate, **17** Antoine et Dominique, **18** Josée Cousin.

à vous! (p.12) **1** David = courageux; Charlie Chaplin = drôle; Tom Pouce = minuscule; Obélix = gros, fort; Astérix = petit, rusé; Peter Pan = jeune; Blanche-Neige = jolie; la belle-mère de Blanche-Neige = jalouse; Attila = cruel; Goliath = grand, fort; Harpagon / Scrooge = avare; Cendrillon = pauvre; les sœurs de Cendrillon = laides; Gargantua = gourmand.
2 *You should have ticked*: jouer au badminton / au basket, danser, chanter, écouter de la musique, aller au cinéma / à la piscine, faire la vaisselle / la cuisine, passer l'aspirateur.

EXERCICES

A 1 Je **porte** des lunettes depuis l'année dernière. *I've been wearing glasses since last year.* **2** J'**apprends** le français depuis trois ans. *I've been learning French for three years.* **3** Nous **avons** une maison de campagne depuis l'an 2000. *We've had a country house since the year 2000.* **4** Vous **habitez** ici depuis longtemps? *Have you been living here long?* **5** Elle **est** en vacances depuis une semaine. *She's been on holiday for a week.* **6** Nous **sommes** à la retraite depuis cinq ans. *We've been retired for five years.* **7** J'**ai** un chien depuis six mois. *I've had a dog for six months.* **8** Vous **jouez** au golf depuis combien de temps? *How long have you been playing golf?* **B** (*Suggested answers*) un professeur intéressant; un enfant curieux; un homme bavard; un problème difficile; un appartement dangereux; un étudiant sérieux; un livre célèbre; un sport élégant; un père patient; un animal rapide; une actrice paresseuse; une voisine aimable; une secrétaire timide; une femme sympathique; une voiture moderne; une question délicate; une cliente indulgente; une histoire ennuyeuse; une remarque intelligente; une vendeuse bilingue.
C (*Suggested answers*) **1** Emmanuel / Emmanuelle, **2** trente, **3** grand / grande, **4** 1 mètre 80, **5** verts, **6** roux, **7** de la voile, **8** aux cartes, **9** au cinéma, **10** au restaurant, **11** toujours de bonne humeur, **12** gentil / gentille, **13** patient / patiente, **14** timide, **15** paresseux / paresseuse.
D (*Suggested answers*) **Lucien Cousin:** Je m'appelle Lucien Cousin. Je suis médecin. J'habite à Fort-de-France à la Martinique. Je suis marié et j'ai 2 enfants qui s'appellent Simon et Annette. Ils ont 12 ans et 9 ans. Je fais de la natation, de la musculation et je joue au tennis. **Tahar Aboulfath:** Je m'appelle Tahar, j'ai vingt-huit **ans et** je suis comptable. Mes parents sont marocains mais moi je suis né à Limoges, donc je suis

beur, comme ma petite amie Yasmin. Nous sortons ensemble depuis six mois. J'habite un petit appartement dans un immeuble moderne. Je fais du taekwondo, des promenades en VTT et du jet-ski qui est un sport très populaire sur les lacs du Limousin. **Claude Dupré:** Je m'appelle Claude Dupré. Je suis fermier. J'habite dans un petit village qui se trouve à 15 km de Rouen en Normandie. Je suis marié. Ma femme s'appelle Liliane. Elle vient de Grenoble dans les Alpes. J'ai 4 enfants, 3 fils: Jean-Pierre qui a 17 ans, Paul qui a 15 ans, Philippe qui a 11 ans et une fille, Colette qui a 13 ans. Ils nous aident pendant les vacances. Mes parents sont à la retraite. Ma mère fait la cuisine pour toute la famille. **Chantal:** Je m'appelle Chantal. J'ai 23 ans. Je suis célibataire mai j'ai un petit ami qui s'appelle Laurent. Il a 25 ans. Je suis vendeuse dans un magasin qui s'appelle Primono. Je prends des cours d'anglais. J'aime aller au cinéma et à la discothèque. J'adore la musique. **Monsieur Déveine:** Je m'appelle Monsieur Déveine. J'habite à Dijon en Bourgogne. Je suis l'ami de Henri Boivin. Je suis marié. Je suis homme d'affaires mais en ce moment je suis au chômage. **E** (*Suggested answer*) Chère Camille, Je t'écris pour te décrire une personne que je viens de rencontrer. C'est la cousine du mari de mon amie Christiane. Elle est grande et maigre et toujours de mauvaise humeur. Elle est toujours fourrée chez le médecin parce qu'elle croit qu'elle est malade. En plus, elle est très bavarde et très curieuse. Elle n'arrête pas de poser des questions indiscrètes! Christiane m'a dit qu'elle est paresseuse et qu'elle n'aide pas son mari à la maison. Elle est aussi très avare. Quand elle est invitée à dîner elle n'apporte ni fleurs, ni bonne bouteille, ni chocolats. Et quand elle a bu quelques verres de vin, elle se dispute avec tout le monde…

écoutez bien! **Numéro de dossier:** 6528, **Nom de famille:** LEGRIS, **Prénom:** Monique, **Âge:** 40 ans, **Situation de famille:** Mariée, **Enfants:** 1 **fils** 2 **fille(s)**, **Couleur des yeux:** Bruns, **Taille:** 1 m 80, **Profession:** Dentiste, **Passe-temps:** Voile, échecs, **Adresse:** 178, avenue de New York, Paris 16ème.

Deuxième unité

avez-vous compris? (p.22) **1** vrai, **2** faux, **3** faux, **4** vrai, **5** vrai, **6** faux, **7** vrai, **8** vrai, **9** faux, **10** vrai, **11** faux, **12** vrai.

à vous! (p.23) **1** aidé, **2** fait, **3** cassé, **4** fait, **5** téléphoné, **6** bavardé, **7** oublié, **8** brûlé, **9** mangé, **10** choisi, **11** mordu, **12** perdu.

avez-vous compris? (p.26) *You should have ticked:* **1** à la tête, bu, **2** des fleurs, des chocolats, **3** au bureau, le réveil, exceptionnel, **4** peur, poissons, effrayant, **5** piqûres, la tension, ennuyeux, **6** toute la journée, désagréable, au cinéma, un mél.

avez-vous compris? (p.28) **1** Madame Roger Coquard, M. et Mme Adrien Portais, **2** Viargues, **3** à Rouen, **4** le samedi 18 mai, **5** Marie-Reine et Jean-Philippe, et Gabrielle, **6** les membres de la famille et les amis proches, **7** à partir de 19 heures, **8** avant le 20 avril, **9** Gabrielle, **10** elle sera aux États-Unis; elle part chez sa sœur à Boston, début mai.

👉 **à vous!** (p.28) **1** une invitation, **2** des vœux pour une personne malade, **3** un mariage, **4** un décès, **5** une naissance.

👉 **à vous!** (p.29) **1** voiture, **2** chemise, **3** sandales, **4** cadeau, **5** train, **6** hélicoptère.

💡 **avez-vous compris?** (p.31) **1** Elle a été malade, **2** au lit, **3** non, elle n'a rien pu manger, **4** non, **5** parce que les Brède ont marié leur fille, **6** splendide, **7** du homard, une sole, du gigot d'agneau, des flageolets, des haricots verts et une pièce montée, **8** l'apéritif, du vin blanc, du vin rouge, du champagne.

👉 **à vous!** (p.31) **1** J'ai passé un dimanche épouvantable. J'ai eu mal à la tête, j'ai dû rester au lit, et je n'ai rien pu manger de la journée. **2** Non. Il me faut un médicament / J'ai besoin d'un médicament pour le foie. **3** J'ai une excuse aujourd'hui. Je suis allé(e) au mariage d'un ami / d'une amie il y a deux jours. **4** Nous avons / on a mangé du homard, puis du gigot d'agneau. J'en ai pris deux fois. **5** Bien sûr! L'apéritif d'abord, puis du vin rouge et du champagne. **6** Pas du tout docteur, mais je compte sur vous pour me donner un bon médicament.

EXERCICES **A** (*Suggested answers*) **1** intéressant, **2** effrayant, **3** désagréable, **4** amusant, **5** exceptionnel, **6** ennuyeux, **7** merveilleux, **8** fatigant, **9** formidable, **10** super. **B** **1** depuis, **2** depuis, **3** il y a, **4** depuis, **5** il y a, **6** depuis, **7** il y a, **8** il y a, **9** depuis, **10** il y a, **11** depuis, **12** il y a, **13** il y a, **14** depuis, **15** depuis. **C** **1** The children didn't play with the neighbours after class. **2** Paul didn't help Mary tidy away her things. **3** Philip didn't wait for Henri outside school. **4** The twins didn't eat. **5** The baby didn't sleep. **6** The dog broke the Chinese vase. **7** I couldn't watch my favourite programme. The TV had broken down. **8** Finally I lost my patience, and I telephoned their mother!

D Cher / Chère Claude, Salut! Je viens de passer la journée à Boulogne. Il a fait très beau. J'ai visité la ville et j'ai pris beaucoup de photos. À midi, j'ai mangé dans un bon restaurant. C'était délicieux! Après, je suis allé(e) à l'hypermarché. J'ai acheté du vin, de la bière et du fromage. À bientôt! Amitiés de … **E 1** Bonjour Jean, comment vas-tu? **2** J'ai téléphoné hier soir. Où es-tu allé? **3** Tu as de la chance. Qu'est ce que vous avez mangé? **4** Qu'avez-vous fait après le repas? **5** Vous avez vu / rencontré des amis?

écoutez bien! **1** Went to disco with his sister and stayed very late. **2** Had a bath, put on a smart dress and went to a restaurant with her boyfriend. **3** Phoned a friend who's been living in Spain for 6 months. Chatted for about 30 minutes. **4** Didn't do anything special. Stayed at home and watched TV from 9 o'clock. An American film, then a programme about England on another channel. **5** Was lucky! Found 50-euro note in the street. Went to the casino and won 1000 euros but lost 600! **6** Went to parents-in-law, argued about politics.

lecture (*Suggested answer*) Jacques Prévert was born in Neuilly-sur-Seine in 1900. When he was young he was part of the surrealist movement and became a poet and brilliant film scriptwriter. In his poetry he speaks about ordinary people and things, but in an unexpected way. Although he has his charming side, he also attacks everything that represents the established order of things, suggesting his own vision of the world and society. He wrote a number of collections of poetry, including *Paroles* and *Histoires*. He also wrote several songs, sung by Yves Montand, and wrote the scripts for a number of films by Marcel Carné, such as *Les Enfants du Paradis* and *Quai des Brumes*. He died in 1977.

In *Le Message* Prévert tells the story of someone who has committed suicide. He uses a series of short sharp similarly constructed sentences for the narrative, so that the reader feels he / she is looking at a sequence of pictures, maybe even cartoon strips. The door that someone opened … The door that someone closed again … The cat that someone stroked … The letter that someone read … The chair that someone overturned … All these are actions in the past that crowd in on one another relentlessly to precipitate the catastrophic event. Then Prévert switches to the present tense to emphasise the immediacy of what is happening, but also perhaps to suggest that this is a common event. The road where someone is still running … The wood that someone is crossing … The river where someone is throwing himself … Then to underline the irreversibility of what has taken place, he returns to the past with the ambiguity of the final phrase. The hospital where someone has died / died / is dead. *L'hôpital où quelqu'un est mort.*

In *Déjeuner du matin* we see an example of how Prévert treats an ordinary subject in an unusual way. It was just a normal breakfast. The person put the coffee, milk and sugar in the cup, then stirred it. He drank it then put the cup down. The repetition of *tasse* and *café* emphasises the banality of the event. Then there is the first hint that something is wrong: *Sans me parler*. With the same precision that he used to pour his cup of coffee, the person lit a cigarette, made smoke

rings and put the ash in the ashtray. *Sans me parler* is repeated. There
follows a series of decisive actions: he got up, he put his hat on his
head, he put on his raincoat because it was raining and set off in the
rain. All this was done without any contact with the other person: *Sans
une parole, Sans me regarder*. The repetition of words such as *pluie*, and
the half rhymes like *parti, pluie, pris*, seem to add to the relentlessness
with which the poem drives to its conclusion. Finally we are left with a
picture of the other person deserted, head in hands in despair, and
crying. … *j'ai pris ma tête dans ma main et j'ai pleuré*. The ordinary
breakfast scene is not just like every other day, but the story of a pre-
meditated event, a turning point perhaps in someone's life.

Troisième unité

avez-vous compris? (p.39) **1** Dijon, **2** la crème de
framboise et la crème de cassis, **3** le kir, **4** la Côte d'Or, **5** bonne table,
bons vins, **6** le bœuf bourguignon, **7** les escargots à la bourguignonne,
8 la région de Chablis, **9** le Palais des Ducs, **10** le Nuits-Saint-Georges.

à vous! (p.39) **Caractéristiques géographiques:**
forêts, lacs, rivières, paysage varié. **Bâtiments d'intérêt historique:**
châteaux, forteresses, abbayes, églises. **Activités sportives:**
sports nautiques, cheval, VTT / vélo /bicyclette, randonnées pédestres.
Autres avantages: cuisine/gastronomie, vins.

avez-vous compris? (p.41) **1** Quelqu'un d'autre, **2** Simon, **3** Colette, **4** Colette, **5** Simon, **6** Simon, **7** Quelqu'un d'autre, **8** Simon, **9** Quelqu'un d'autre, **10** Simon, **11** Quelqu'un d'autre, **12** Colette, **13** Simon, **14** Quelqu'un d'autre, **15** Colette.

avez-vous compris? (p.43) Corsica is not very far from France and you can be sure to get good weather. There are lots of things to do and see although there are not too many tourists yet. The coast is beautiful and perfect for seaside holidays. You can also find a deserted creek if you go by boat. The mountains are ideal for hiking and horse riding. There are lots of historic places and the food is different.

à vous! (p.44) **1** située, **2** population, **3** climat, **4** près, **5** adorent, **6** cher, **7** clients, **8** fiers.

avez-vous compris? (p.45) **1** vrai, **2** vrai, **3** faux, **4** vrai, **5** faux, **6** vrai, **7** vrai, **8** faux, **9** vrai, **10** vrai.

avez-vous compris? (p.47) **1** Villes commerciales et industrielles / Circulation, bruit, pollution / Université / Monuments historiques (cathédrale, maisons pittoresques etc.) / tramway. **2** The flat is modern, comfortable, away from the town centre. There is a lift, a digital code and intercom system. There is a large living room and a guest room.

à vous! (p.48) **1** a (vi), b (vii), c (x), d (ii), e (ix), f (iii), g (viii), h (iv), i (v), j (i). **2 a** lu, **b** vu, **c** visités, **d** regardée, **e** bue, **f** goûtées, **g** photographiée, **h** mangé.

avez-vous compris? (p.49)   **1** appartement grand standing, **2** entrée, **3** agencé / remis entièrement à neuf, **4** meublé, **5** place de parking, **6** vide-ordures, **7** cheminée, **8** cave et grenier.

avez-vous compris? (p.50)   **1** maison ancienne, **2** cuisine équipée / aménagée, **3** bureau, **4** salle de jeux, **5** terrasse, **6** chauffage central, **7** chaumière, **8** abri et serre, **9** sous-sol, **10** rez-de-chaussée, **11** arrière-cuisine, **12** moquette, **13** dépendances, **14** salle d'eau / cabinet de toilette, **15** jardin paysager, **16** studio indépendant.

avez-vous compris? (p.51)   Ad 3603 is nearest to Guillaume's requirements. It includes a small fitted kitchen, a bathroom and a bedroom. It is furnished with a settee, a desk and a bed.

EXERCICES   **A** **1** des, **2** des, **3** de, **4** des, **5** de, **6** de, **7** d', **8** des. **B** **1** que, **2** qui, **3** qui, **4** que, **5** qu', **6** qu', **7** qui, **8** qui. **C** **1** la semaine dernière, **2** déménagé, **3** perdu, **4** cherchées, **5** trouvées, **6** en ville, **7** des meubles, **8** ma chambre, **9** fauteuils, **10** dormi, **11** répondu, **12** tes nouvelles. **D** **1** qui, qui, oiseau, **2** qui, qu', poisson, **3** dont, chat, **4** qui, chien, **5** que, araignée, **6** qu', qui, licorne, **7** que, mouton, **8** dont, dont, requin, **9** qui, phénix, **10** dont, qui, girafe.

écoutez bien!   **Advantages / Drawbacks 1 Hotel:** in old picturesque district / problems with plumbing (no hot water). **2 Food:** nice specialities; lots of good cheap restaurants / has put on weight (2kg). **3 Weather:** nice, very hot / got sunburnt. **4 Beach & Sea:** beautiful beach; warm sea / sharks.

5 Places of interest: lots to see: castle; museum, park / full of tourists.
6 Shopping: great souvenir shops; original things to buy / very expensive; has run out of money.

lecture *(Suggested answer)* **1** Buy local produce that has been grown outside. It is better than fruit and vegetables grown under glass and has not had to travel so far. Compost the waste. **2** Put lids on pans when you cook. **3** Do not use running water to rinse vegetables or wash up. Use surplus water on plants and also collect rainwater. **4** Turn off taps when you wash or brush your teeth. Have a shower rather than a bath, but do not leave the water running while you soap yourself. **5** Use the eco programme on your washing machine or dishwasher. Do a full load. Dry clothes on a line rather than in the dryer. Defrost the freezer regularly. **6** Improve insulation in your house – double-glazing, loft insulation etc. **7** If you need to change your heating system, choose renewable energy such as solar or wind. **8** Do not leave the TV or DVD player on stand-by. Switch off. **9** Use natural household products such as vinegar or wax. **10** Sort, re-use, and re-cycle paper, glass, plastic etc. **11** Put a notice on your door saying no advertising. **12** Instead of watching TV, read or play games for three hours.

Faites le point! (unités 1–3)

1 a3, b6, c9, d1, e8, f4, g7, h2, i5. **2** ai vendu, ai pu, ai mangé, ai beaucoup grossi, ai visité, ai perdu, n'ai pas dormi, écrit, plu, ouvert, pris. **3** **a** mises, **b** que / trouvées, **c** vues, **d** rendus, **e** qui / vendu / veut. **4** **a** bue (le Nuits-Saint-Georges), **b** préparée (la tarte à l'oignon), **c** choisi (le Sylvaner), **d** faite (les crêpes), **e** acheté (le camembert), **f** mangé (la bouillabaisse). **5** grand / grande – petit / petite; beau / belle – laid / laide; patient / patiente – impatient / impatiente; mince – gros / grosse; jeune – vieux / vieille; marié / mariée – célibataire; long / longue – court / courte; intéressant / intéressante – ennuyeux / ennuyeuse; vieux / vieille – moderne; bonne humeur – mauvaise humeur; généreux / généreuse – égoïste; riche – pauvre; courageux / courageuse – timide; doué / douée – nul / nulle. **6 a** des plages magnifiques, **b** des ruelles pittoresques, **c** une église du douzième siècle, **d** un endroit isolé, **e** un vieux quartier, **f** un vieil immeuble, **g** un jardin paysager, **h** une station balnéaire très connue, **i** une cuisine aménagée, **j** un château du Moyen Âge, **k** une maison ancienne, **l** une jolie rivière. **7** (*Suggested answers*) **a** Je suis de taille moyenne (Je mesure 1 mètre 65). Je suis brune. J'ai les cheveux courts. J'ai les yeux verts. Je suis très jalouse et plutôt têtue. **b** Je suis petit et gros. Je suis gourmand. Je suis toujours de bonne humeur mais je suis plutôt paresseux. **c** Je suis grande et assez mince. Je suis blonde et j'ai les yeux bleus. J'ai les cheveux longs. Je suis jolie, intelligente et célibataire. **d** J'ai dix-huit ans. Je suis très grand (Je mesure 2 mètres!). J'ai les cheveux noirs et les yeux marron. Je suis sympathique mais assez timide. **8 a** The rooms face south, there's a terrace, sea view and direct access to the beach, equipped kitchen and bathroom. **b** Tennis courts, swimming pools, keep-fit obstacle course, table tennis, bowls. **c** Two days free of charge. **d** It depends if there are places available. **e** By asking for your home and office phone numbers. **f** The bedrooms and living room. **g** They're close to shops, car park and the métro, and they overlook a park. **h** No. You can go to the sales office on Saturdays and Mondays, but at other times you must make an appointment. **i** Immediately. **j** You are supposed to send your visiting card.

k Living room, 1 bedroom, kitchen, bathroom and toilet. **l** 5th
m No. There is a lift. **n** Yes. It has been renovated. **o** By central heating.
p It also has a garage, a balcony and a beautiful view.

Quatrième unité

 avez-vous compris? (p.62)   1L, 2L, 3C, 4C, 5L, 6C, 7L, 8C, 9C, 10L.

à vous! (p.63)   **1** J'ai réservé une table pour deux personnes par téléphone ce matin. **2** Merci. Deux menus à vingt-six euros s'il vous plaît. **3** Je prendrai l'avocat aux crevettes. **4** Non, les asperges vinaigrette. Il / elle est allergique aux crevettes. **5** Le poulet rôti / Un steak / Le lapin / L'omelette. **6** Qu'est-ce que vous recommandez?

avez-vous compris? (p.65)   **1** Oui, ils ont dû attendre longtemps. **2** Oui, il y avait du monde. **3** Elle a commandé les crêpes Suzette. **4** Citron givré, moka, mousse au chocolat, gâteau norvégien. **5** Le gâteau norvégien était en supplément. **6** Elle a vu le dessert appétissant de la dame à la table d'à côté.

à vous! (p.65)   **1 a** fourchette / elle est sale, **b** verre / il est fêlé, **c** assiette / elle est ébréchée, **d** serviette / elle est tachée, **e** couteau / il ne coupe pas bien, **f** nappe / elle n'est pas repassée, **g** fleurs / elles sont fanées, **h** carafe d'eau / elle n'est pas fraîche, **i** baguette / elle est rassie, **j** bouteille de vin / elle est vide.

2 a (xii), **b** (xi), **c** (xiii), **d** (iv), **e** (viii), **f** (i), **g** (iii), **h** (vi), **i** (x), **j** (ii), **k** (vii), **l** (v), **m** (ix).

avez-vous compris? (p.67)   **1** Le palais de justice, la cathédrale, le Gros-Horloge. **2** Elle préfère le Gros Horloge et la cathédrale. **3** Elle se sert souvent de la sauce normande. **4** Elle adore les soles de Dieppe et les crustacés. **5** Les tripes à la mode de Caen. **6** Le cidre et le calvados. **7** Le camembert, le livarot, le pont l'évêque. **8** Le fromage de chèvre. **9** Non. En général elle passe ses vacances en France. **10** C'est la Normandie qu'elle aime le mieux.

à vous! (p.68)   **1** une pomme de pin, **2** un œillet, **3** les Maltais, **4** les mocassins, **5** l'eau d'Évian, **6** pomme.

avez-vous compris? (p.71)   **1** Chantal, **2** l'étudiante, **3** la grand-mère, **4** le traiteur, **5** la mère de l'étudiante, **6** Chantal, **7** l'étudiante, **8** Chantal, **9** le traiteur, **10** la mère de l'étudiante, **11** Chantal, **12** la grand-mère, **13** la mère de l'étudiante, **14** Chantal, **15** la grand-mère, **16** l'étudiante, **17** le traiteur, **18** Chantal.

à vous! (p.72)   une bonne cuisinière, des plats cuisinés, ouvrir une boîte de conserve, faire réchauffer au micro-ondes, c'est bon pour la ligne, faire la cuisine, pour des raisons d'argent et d'hygiène, un régime équilibré, des recettes basses calories, prendre son temps, des produits surgelés, des petits plats.

EXERCICES **A** **1** lequel / celui, **2** dont, **3** que, **4** dont, **5** qui, **6** dont, **7** lesquels / ceux-ci, **8** qui. **B** **1** laquelle, **2** lequel, **3** lesquels, **4** lequel, **5** lesquelles. **C** **1** Deux menus à trente-six euros s'il vous plaît. **2** Qu'est-ce que c'est la soupe du jour? **3** Une soupe et un melon au porto. **4** Le lapin pour ma femme, et pour moi / moi, je prendrai le poulet rôti. Avec quoi le servez-vous? **5** Qu'est-ce que vous recommandez pour accompagner le poulet? **6** Alors, une bouteille de Chablis. **7** (*Suggested answer*) Une crème caramel et un baba au rhum. **D** **1** végétarienne, **2** recettes, **3** régime, **4** ligne, **5** cuisinés, **6** micro-ondes, **7** frais, **8** conserves, **9** produits, **10** emballage. **E** **1 a** Le Pub Irlandais, **b** La Bonne Taverne, **c** Chez Bébert, **d** Le panier de coquillages, **e** La Bonne Fourchette, **f** Happy Hour. **2 a** jusqu'à 2 heures du matin, **b** tous les jours / sept jours sur sept (7/7), **c** service en continu, **d** à partir de 11 heures, **e** à deux pas de …, **f** au cœur de la ville, **g** vin et café compris.

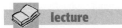 **écoutez bien!** **Première partie: la télérecette** **1** 4, **2** 100, **3** verre, **4** 150, **5** deux, **6** trois, **7** café, **8** œufs, **9** blancs / jaunes, **10** jaunes / blancs, **11** sucre, **12** crème fraîche, **13** frigidaire, **14** heures. **Deuxième partie: au restaurant** 18, champignons, rôti de porc, ratatouille, pâtisseries (babas au rhum, mille-feuilles, éclairs), vin rosé. She's afraid to eat mushrooms, she's a vegetarian, she's on a diet and she doesn't like rosé wine. 18 euros is too much for ratatouille!

lecture **1** R, **2** A, **3** M, **4** R, **5** A, **6** M, **7** A, **8** M, **9** R, **10** A, **11** R, **12** M + A.

Cinquième unité

avez-vous compris? (p.82)   *You should have ticked*:
1 charcuterie, **2** a oublié ses lunettes. **3** au fond du magasin, **4** du shampooing, des savonnettes, **5** d'ampoules, **6** n'a pas assez d'argent, **7** attendre sa fille.

à vous! (p.82)   CHARCUTERIE, 1 saucisson sec, 4 tranches de jambon; ÉPICERIE, 1 kilo de sucre, 1 boîte de céréales, 2 paquets de café; COSMÉTIQUES, 1 tube de dentifrice, 3 savonnettes; LIBRAIRIE-PAPETERIE, un journal, 1 paquet d'enveloppes; BOISSONS, 12 boîtes de bière, 1 bouteille de vin, SURGELÉS, 1 pot de glace, un paquet de petits pois surgelés; CONFISERIE, 1 œuf de Pâques, 1 paquet de bonbons; BOULANGERIE, 2 baguettes, 1 grand paquet de croissants; ÉLECTRO-MÉNAGER, 1 robot ménager, 2 ampoules; VÊTEMENTS-HOMMES, une chemise; PRODUITS D'ENTRETIEN, 1 boîte de lessive; FRUITS ET LÉGUMES, un poivron, une botte d'asperges, 1 sac de pommes de terre, 1 kilo de pêches; BOUCHERIE, 6 côtelettes d'agneau; CRÉMERIE, dix yaourts nature, 1 pot de crème fraîche, 1 demi-livre de beurre, 1 litre de lait demi-écrémé, 1 douzaine d'œufs, 1 camembert; VÊTEMENTS-FEMMES, 3 paires de collants, 1 jupe; SPORT, une raquette de tennis, 1 paire de baskets.

avez-vous compris? (p.85)   **1** Deux fois par semaine, **2** C'est plus sympathique et elle y rencontre ses amies. **3** Avec les commerçants. **4** Il y a un très grand choix. **5** Oui, c'est moins cher qu'au supermarché. **6** Elle aime goûter. **7** Faire la queue à la caisse. **8** Elle porte un imper avec une capuche et des bottes en caoutchouc.

avez-vous compris? (p.86) On peut se garer sans problème. On trouve tout sous le même toit. Les produits sont de bonne qualité. Tout est propre et emballé. C'est meilleur marché que les petits magasins. On peut payer par chèque ou avec une carte de crédit.

à vous! (p.86) **1** la queue, **2** le caddie / chariot, **3** il pleut, **4** besoin, **5** une enquête, **6** se garer, **7** souvent, **8** partageons, **9** connais, **10** concurrence, **11** par semaine, **12** argent liquide, **13** goûter, **14** les chariots / caddies, **15** viens.

avez-vous compris? (p.89) **1** poste, **2** emballé, **3** livre, **4** cadeau, **5** recettes, **6** s'intéresse, **7** colis / paquet, **8** cher, **9** remplir, **10** acheté, **11** carnet, **12** autocollants.

à vous! (p.89) **1** d, **2** b, **3** c, **4** a.

avez-vous compris? (p.91) **1** Angleterre, **2** vacances, **3** travailler, **4** stage, **5** entreprise, **6** anglais, **7** compte courant, **8** carte de crédit, **9** régler, **10** distributeurs automatiques (de billets).

à vous! (p.91) **1** d, **2** c, **3** b, **4** a.

avez-vous compris? (p.93) **1** Ils sont arrivés en voiture. **2** Trois hommes sont descendus de voiture. **3** Le quatrième est resté au volant. **4** Ils sont entrés dans la banque vers onze heures et demie. **5** Ils en sont sortis environ cinq minutes plus tard. **6** Oui. **7** Parce qu'il n'est pas James Bond.

avez-vous compris? (p.94)   La jeune cliente était à **la banque**. Elle a entendu **du bruit** derrière elle, et quand elle a regardé, elle a vu **trois** hommes. L'un d'eux a dit, 'Haut les **mains**! Que personne ne **bouge**!' Ensuite ils sont allés droit **à la caisse**, où ils ont menacé **la caissière**. Ils lui ont demandé de mettre tout **l'argent** dans de **grands** sacs. Le gros cambrioleur avait les cheveux **noirs** et le **jeune** portait un bonnet en **laine** et un pull **à rayures**.

à vous! (p.98)   **2** Je suis arrivé(e) à … **3** Trois. **4** À onze heures et quart peut-être / À environ onze heures et quart. **5** Oui, ils ont sorti leur revolver. **6** Ils sont allés droit à la caisse. **7** Ils lui ont demandé de mettre l'argent dans de grands sacs. **8** (*Suggested answer*) Moi, je n'ai rien fait.

EXERCICES

A 1h, 2f, 3j, 4b, 5l, 6e, 7a, 8k, 9c, 10i, 11g, 12d.
B (*Suggested answer*) **1** Un carnet de timbres, s'il vous plaît. **2** Je voudrais envoyer un colis. **3** En recommandé, ce sont des documents très importants. **4** Le colis va arriver quand? **5** La boîte aux lettres est dehors? **C** **1** sommes allés, **2** sommes partis, **3** avons trouvé, **4** sommes descendus, **5** sommes allés, **6** travailler, **7** ouvrir, **8** virer, **9** utiliser, **10** régler, **11** retirer, **12** sommes ressortis, **13** suis entré(e), **14** est resté. **D** 1, 5, 10, 4, 12, 9, 3, 7, 11, 2, 6, 8. **E** (*Suggested answer*) Cher Jean / Chère Jeanne, Merci beaucoup pour le livre de recettes françaises que je viens de recevoir. Il est arrivé ce matin. Vous êtes très gentil(le) d'avoir pensé à moi et de l'avoir envoyé pour mon anniversaire. Je vais m'en servir aujourd'hui même pour préparer une spécialité provençale. J'ai invité des amis à dîner ce soir. Je vais vous écrire plus longuement bientôt. Amitiés, …

écoutez bien! Première partie 1 20%, garden furniture, **2** camemberts, dairy, **3** parents, information office, **4** three, second birthday, **5** ten, check-outs.

Deuxième partie

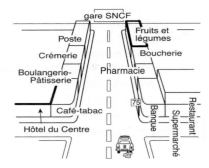

Sixième unité

avez-vous compris? (p.101)   **1** G, **2** un(e) employé(e) de l'Office de Tourisme, **3** G, P, **4** G, P, **5** G, P, **6** G, **7** P, **8** G, P, **9** G, P, **10** un fermier.

avez-vous compris? (p.103)   **1** V, **2** F, **3** F, **4** V, **5** V, **6** F, **7** V, **8** F

avez-vous compris? (p.104)   **1** piles, **2** sac à dos, **3** mouillés, **4** trempés, **5** une lampe de poche, **6** à plat.

à vous! (p.104)   **1** ils ont traversé, **2** ils n'ont pas campé, **3** ils ont eu froid, **4** ils n'ont pas survolé, **5** ils ont vu, **6** ils ont grimpé, **7** ils sont allés, **8** ils ont visité, **9** ils ont passé, **10** ils ne sont pas allés.

avez-vous compris? (p.105)   Oui: **2, 5, 7, 9, 10, 12**. Non: **4, 7**. *Erreurs:* **1** Non, il n'a pas fait beau / il a fait mauvais / il a fait un temps épouvantable. **3** Si, ils ont dû / il leur a fallu louer des draps. **6** Non, ils n'ont pas joué au tennis et au foot, ils ont joué au tennis de table et au baby-foot. **8** Non. Elle attire beaucoup de visiteurs à Bayeux. / Le musée du débarquement attire beaucoup de visiteurs à Arromanches. **11** Si, ils ont trouvé le musée très intéressant.

à vous! (p.106)   (*Suggested answer*) Allô! … Oui … Salut, Paul! Ça va? … Où êtes-vous? … Quel temps fait-il? … Vous faites toujours du camping? … Qu'est-ce que vous avez fait le soir? … Ça vous plaît, l'auberge de jeunesse? … Il y a des étrangers? … Vous êtes allés à Bayeux? … Vous avez vu la tapisserie? … Qu'est-ce que tu en penses? … Il y avait beaucoup de touristes? … Vous avez fait les plages du débarquement? … Où est-ce? … Qu'est-ce que vous avez fait là-bas? … C'était intéressant? … Vous avez vu des cimetières militaires? … Qu'est-ce que vous allez faire maintenant? … Alors, au revoir!

avez-vous compris? (p.108)   **Shopping / Nourriture:** bar-restaurant, dépôt de pain. **Les équipements du terrain:** emplacements ombragés, branchements électriques, blocs

sanitaires, points d'eau chaude, bacs pour la vaisselle, machine à laver.
Ce qu'il y a pour les jeunes: piscine, aire de jeux, tables de ping-pong
et de billard. **Les environs:** plage de sable, centre équestre, Porto-
Vecchio, Bonifacio, forêt.

à vous! (p.109)   **1 a** (ii), **b** (viii), **c** (i), **d** (xi), **e** (vi), **f** (iv),
g (v), **h** (x), **i** (xii), **j** (ix), **k** (iii), **l** (vii). **2 a** terrain de camping,
b emplacements, **c** branchements, **d** blocs sanitaires, **e** prises-rasoir,
f machine à laver, **g** vaisselle, **h** magasins, **i** dépôts, **j** plats à emporter,
k bar-restaurant, **l** piscine, **m** aire de jeux, **n** plages, **o** centre équestre.

avez-vous compris? (p.111)   **1** La famille Dupré veut
aller faire du camping pendant **une semaine en juillet**. **2** Si on ne veut
pas faire la cuisine, on peut **acheter des plats cuisinés à emporter**. **3**
On peut acheter à manger **midi et soir tous les jours**. **4** Des
machines à laver et des séchoirs à linge sont à la disposition des
campeurs. **5** En plus de l'emplacement, il faut payer la redevance
campeur et une **taxe de séjour**. **6** Si vous voulez réserver, vous devez
remplir un formulaire et **envoyer** des arrhes. **7** Les **conditions de
réservation, d'annulation et de remboursement** figurent au dos de
la confirmation de réservation.

à vous! (p.112)   **1** un emplacement, **2** 8 au 15, **3** service
de plats cuisinés à emporter, **4** midi et soir, **5** sèche-linge / séchoirs à
linge, **6** 10 euros, **7** la redevance campeur, **8** les enfants de moins de 3
ans, **9** un formulaire, **10** d'arrhes.

EXERCICES   **A** 1g, 2j, 3a, 4e, 5b, 6i, 7d, 8f, 9c, 10h.
B 1 Je suis allé(e) en Bretagne avec des amis. On est arrivés vendredi soir. **2** Samedi, il a plu toute la journée. **3** Le matin on est allés à la piscine et l'après-midi on a visité un château. **4** Non, on est restés à l'hôtel. **5** On a fait de la voile. **6** On est partis à seize heures / quatre heures de l'après-midi et je suis rentré(e) / arrivé(e) à la maison à vingt heures / huit heures du soir. **7** C'était super / formidable / génial!
C 1 suis rentré, **2** suis parti, **3** a campé, **4** a couché, **5** a plu, **6** a dû, **7** a grimpé, **8** ai pris, **9** a aussi visité, **10** a traversé, **11** a vu, **12** est allé(s).
D (*Suggested answer*) Monsieur, Je voudrais réserver un emplacement pour une caravane dans votre terrain de camping, du 5 au 19 août inclus. J'aimerais savoir s'il y a un restaurant, un magasin d'alimentation ou si vous faites des plats à emporter. Y a-t-il une piscine et une aire de jeux pour les enfants? Nous avons un chien. Acceptez-vous les animaux? Y a-t-il des branchements électriques, des points d'eau chaude et des facilités pour faire la lessive et la vaisselle? Quels sont vos tarifs? Est-il nécessaire de réserver et faut-il envoyer des arrhes? Je vous serais reconnaissant(e) de m'envoyer tous renseignements utiles à l'adresse suivante: **E A** 5, 10, 8. **B** 7, 3, 9. **C** 14, 1, 15, 6. **D** 4, 11. **E** 2, 12, 13.
F (*Suggested answer*) Par un beau matin ensoleillé, Nicole et moi sommes partis en week-end. Après avoir dit au revoir à notre famille, nous sommes montés à vélo. Sur notre porte-bagage il y avait une tente et des sacs de couchage. Tout à coup, il a commencé à pleuvoir. Alors nous avons décidé de descendre à l'hôtel. Une heure plus tard, nous sommes arrivés à un croisement où nous avons dû décider quel chemin prendre. Nous sommes enfin arrivés au centre-ville où nous avons passé la nuit. Le lendemain matin nous avons acheté des provisions. Nous

sommes repartis vers dix heures du matin et nous avons pris la direction du camping *Belle Vue*. Il y avait déjà un monde fou. Peu après notre arrivée, j'ai monté la tente avec difficulté tandis que Nicole a pris un bain de soleil. Puis j'ai fait cuire des brochettes et des saucisses. Il a fait beau toute la journée et Nicole a attrapé un coup de soleil. Elle a mis de la crème calmante et elle est allée au lit tôt. Je n'étais pas content, mais je lui a dit 'Pauvre Nicole'.

écoutez bien!

Section A: Ajaccio – 3, Porto – 4, Evisa – 2, Calvi – 1. **Section B:** Saint-Florent – 5, Bastia – 4, Asco – 1, Cervione – 3, Aléria – 2. **Section C:** Porto-Vecchio – 2, Bonifacio – 3, Plateau de Cauria – 1, Propriano – 2.

lecture

1 It is situated in the south of the island, where the nicest beaches are to be found. **2** It has 150 spaces. **3** It has hot showers, restaurants, children's play areas. You can hire camping and beach equipment and mountain bikes. **4** Watersports: swimming in the sea, windsurfing, diving, jet-ski and hobby-cat. Others: cycling, tennis, volley-ball and pétanque, a type of bowls game. **5** Old ruins, distilleries, petrified trees, small islands … **6** Pitches for people with their own tent or caravan, tents, tents with camping equipment, caravans.

Faites le point! (unités 4–6)

1 a la sole meunière, **b** la bibliothèque, **c** du dentifrice, **d** l'emballage, **e** de la lessive, **f** le rayon confiserie. **2 1g** I reserved a table for three by telephone. **2c** Are you ready to order, ladies and gentlemen? **3h** What do you recommend? **4f** What do you serve it with? **5i** I'll have the 16-euro menu. **6e** I am allergic to shellfish. **7a** To start with I'll have the fish soup. **8b** We are vegetarians. **9d** The cake is really appetising! **3 a** Je vais à l'étranger le mois prochain. **b** En Angleterre. J'y vais pour travailler. **c** Oui, c'est ça / exact. Est-ce qu'on peut / Peut-on / On peut utiliser les cartes de crédit françaises? **d** J'ai une carte bleue. **e** Est-ce qu'on peut / Peut-on / On peut retirer de l'argent aux distributeurs de billets? **f** Est-ce qu'on peut / Peut-on / On peut utiliser la carte de la même manière qu'en France? **4** Quand elle **est allée** en Normandie, elle **a fait** du camping. Elle **a monté** sa tente toute seule. Elle **a eu** de la chance, car il **a fait** très beau. Elle **est arrivée** début juin, et elle **est restée** trois semaines. Elle **a passé** de très bonnes vacances, et elle **a pleuré** quand elle **est rentrée** chez elle. **5 a** Je suis allé(e) en France. **b** J'y suis allé(e) tout(e) seul(e). **c** Non, je suis allé(e) près de Tours. **d** Non, je suis descendu(e) / allé(e) à l'hôtel. **e** J'y suis resté(e) une semaine, puis j'ai passé deux jours à Paris. **f** J'ai visité beaucoup de châteaux et j'ai joué au golf. **g** Bien sûr. Je suis allé(e) au cinéma, au concert et au restaurant. **h** J'ai passé de bonnes vacances mais je voudrais visiter une autre région. **6 a** LA MARÉE, because it is close to the sea and has plenty of facilities, free hot water, heated toilet blocks, take-away meals, and also activities for the children, swimming pool, games and TV. **b** LA MOTTE, because it is by the sea, in a semi-shady position, with a launching ramp for boats. It also has hot water and a launderette. **c** LE CLAIR DE LUNE, because there are take-away meals, and dogs are not allowed. **d** LES PINS, because it is a small friendly site, and dogs are accepted.

Septième unité

avez-vous compris? (p.125) **1** triste, **2** petit ami, **3** la soirée, **4** feuilleton, **5** enregistré, **6** émission humoristique, **7** rater, **8** rire, **9** dîner, **10** DVD.

à vous! (p.125) 1e, 2k, 3h, 4c, 5a, 6j, 7g, 8l, 9d, 10b, 11i, 12f.

avez-vous compris? (p.128) 1d, 2f, 3e, 4a, 5b, 6c.

avez-vous compris? (p.129) **1** vrai, **2** on ne sait pas, **3** faux, **4** vrai, **5** vrai, **6** faux.

à vous! (p.130) **1** Qu'est-ce que vous avez fait après être rentré à la maison? **2** Qu'est-ce que vous avez fait après avoir téléphoné à vos parents? **3** Qu'est-ce que vous avez fait après être allé à la station service? **4** Qu'est-ce que vous avez fait après avoir bavardé avec votre amie? **5** Qu'est -ce que vous avez fait après être allée au supermarché? **6** Qu'est-ce que vous avez fait après avoir pris une douche?

avez-vous compris? (p.132) 5, 7, 3, 1, 4, 8, 2, 6.

à vous! (p.133) **1** Elle s'est réveillée tôt / de bonne heure. **2** Elle s'est levée tout de suite. **3** Elle a mis son maillot de bain. **4** Elle est allée faire sa séance de natation. **5** Elle a plongé dans la piscine. **6** Elle ne s'est pas noyée parce qu'elle sait nager / Elle a nagé.

avez-vous compris? (p.134) **1** Anna Belle s'est disputée avec son mari. **4** Elle a entendu la voiture de Jean quand il est sorti. **7** C'est Jean, le mari, qui a découvert l'accident.

avez-vous compris? (p.135) **1** Anna s'est couchée à dix heures. **2** Avant de s'endormir, elle a pris des somnifères. **3** Elle s'est réveillée tôt comme d'habitude. **4** Elle a fait vingt longueurs. **5** Jean et Anna se sont disputés avant de se coucher. **6** Jean nie la dispute avec sa femme.

à vous! (p.135) **1** Qu'est-ce que vous avez fait avant de vous changer? **2** Qu'est-ce que vous avez fait avant de téléphoner à vos parents? **3** Qu'est-ce que vous avez fait avant de boire un café? **4** Qu'est-ce que vous avez fait avant de prendre une douche? **5** Qu'est-ce que vous avez fait avant de vous reposer? **6** Qu'est-ce que vous avez fait avant de manger une pomme?

avez-vous compris? (p.138) **1** Véronique, **2** Jean, **3** Véronique, **4** Guy, **5** Jean, **6** Véronique, **7** Véronique, **8** Jean, **9** Jean, **10** Guy, **11** Véronique, **12** Jean, **13** Véronique, **14** Guy, **15** Jean.

à vous! (p.139) **1** rencontrés, **2** mariés, **3** disputés, **4** couchée, **5** sorti, **6** entendu, **7** couché, **8** rentré, **9** dirigé, **10** levée, **11** préparé, **12** venue, **13** inquiétée, **14** trouvé, **15** tué.

EXERCICES   **A 1** Qu'est-ce qu'on joue (en ce moment)? **2** J'en ai entendu parler. C'est en anglais? **3** C'est à quelle heure? **4** Où est-ce qu'on se retrouve? **5** D'accord / Parfait. À ce soir (alors)! **B** **1** Je me suis couché(e) vers minuit. **2** Nous nous sommes disputés à cause des enfants. **3** Je me suis endormi(e) parce qu'c'était ennuyeux! **4** Nous nous sommes cachés derrière un arbre. **5** Nous nous sommes baignés dans la piscine de l'hôtel. **6** Oui, nous nous sommes mariés le 25 exactement. **7** Non, je me suis levé(e) à midi. **8** Nous nous sommes rencontrés il y a 6 mois, en Espagne. **C** **1** J'ai fait des courses. **2** Je me suis réveillé(e) à sept heures et je me suis levé(e) tout de suite, comme d'habitude. **3** Je suis allé(e) en ville. **4** Non, j'ai pris le train. **5** Non, avec des amis. Nous nous sommes / On s'est retrouvés à la gare. **6** Oui, mais je suis rentré(e) tard (à la maison) et j'étais fatigué(e). **7** Je me suis endormi(e) devant la télé.

lecture **A** **1** 1.2 million. **2** In 1977. **3** In ruins and covered with nettles. **4** It is the largest night-time production in the world, using the most recent technology, special effects and the enthusiasm of over 3000 actors. **5** 23 hectares. **6** 1,100 actors. **7** 5,000. **8** Just 28. **9** June to September. **10** From the Middle Ages to the end of the Second World War (700 years). **B** **1** Le Bourg 1900, **2** Les Vikings, **3** La Bataille du Donjon, **4** Le Village XVIIIème, **5** Le Bal des Oiseaux Fantômes, **6** La Cité Médiévale.

(Suggested Answer) **1** In a market town of the 1900s you can plunge into the warm atmosphere of the shops, hear the rural policeman give advice to the people and watch automated figures of musicians start up in the windows. **2** You can see the fierce warriors from the north rise up out of the water and flames to interrupt a wedding. They attack the peaceful fort of 2000 and battle rages at the foot of the watchtower. **3** You are invited to the celebration of chivalry at Puy du Fou. Suddenly great war machines appear and the keep becomes the scene of a fierce

battle. Tricks and fights on horseback, cascades are all part of it. **4** You can join in the happy atmosphere in the village and meet the craftsmen, potters, blacksmiths, cabinet-makers. Near the washing-place you will be swept along into a wild dance by the enticing sound of traditional musicians. **5** Haunting memories come back to you from the ruins of the castle, as dozens of birds of prey rise from the ghostly dovecote and the forgotten deep. **6** Cross the drawbridge and in the fortified enclosure you can find all the richness of the Middle Ages and the skill of the craftsmen. At the foot of the ramparts let yourself be charmed by the tricks of the Minstrel Magician.

écoutez bien! **1** Jean-Pierre est monté au premier. **10** Il a allumé la télé. **9** Il s'est disputé avec la personne qui lui a téléphoné et il a raccroché, en colère. **8** Il a répondu. **4** Il s'est déshabillé et il a pris une douche. **11** Il s'est servi un whisky 'on ze rocks'. **7** Jean-Pierre est descendu au rez-de-chaussée. **3** Il s'est brossé les dents. **12** Il s'est assis dans un fauteuil confortable … et il s'est endormi. **6** Tout à coup, le téléphone a sonné. **2** Il a ouvert la porte de la salle de bains, il a allumé puis il a refermé la porte. **5** Il a chanté.

Huitième unité

avez-vous compris? (p.147) **1** La patience. **2** Parce que c'est un métier très fatigant. **3** Les sixièmes. **4** C'est un âge difficile. **5** Une trentaine. **6** 8 heures – 5 ou 6 heures. **7** Faire les cours, corriger les copies, préparer les leçons, aller à des réunions, voir les parents d'élèves. **8** Ils ont besoin de vacances.

👉 **à vous!** (p.147) 1h, 2g, 3e, 4f, 5c, 6d, 7b, 8a.

💡 **avez-vous compris?** (p.149) **1** vrai, **2** faux, **3** vrai, **4** faux, **5** vrai, **6** vrai, **7** faux, **8** faux.

👉 **à vous!** (p.149) **1** un métier, **2** dur, **3** la mer, **4** compte, **5** vie, **6** il faut, **7** s'occuper.

💡 **avez-vous compris?** (p.150) **1** vrai, **2** faux, **3** vrai, **4** vrai, **5** faux, **6** vrai, **7** faux.

👉 **à vous!** (p.151) **1 a** inconvénients, **b** le contact, **c** la vie de famille, **d** assez fatigant. **2** (*Suggested answer*) **Jeanne a** Je suis professeur. **b** Ça dépend, mais les cours commencent à huit heures du matin. **c** Ça dépend aussi, mais les cours finissent à cinq heures. **d** À part les cours, je corrige les copies, je prépare les leçons, je vais à des réunions et je vois des parents d'élèves. **e** J'ai beaucoup de temps libre. J'ai des vacances à la fin de chaque trimestre et les grandes vacances l'été. **f** C'est épuisant. **g** En général, les jeunes sont gentils. **Yves a** Je suis marin-pêcheur. **b** Je commence à une heure du matin. **c** Ça dépend, en fin d'après-midi. **d** Après le retour au port, il faut vendre la pêche et s'occuper du bateau. **e** Tous les week-ends. **f** C'est très dur et c'est dangereux quand il fait mauvais temps. **g** J'adore la mer et comme je travaille à mon compte, je gagne bien ma vie. **La serveuse a** Je suis serveuse dans un restaurant qui ne sert que des plats à base de

poissons et de fruits de mer. **b** Je commence à 10 heures du matin.
c Vers minuit ou une heure du matin. **d** Je sers, naturellement, je mets
le couvert, je prépare les apéritifis, je fais les glaçons, les cafés, je
prépare les additions. **e** Deux jours par semaine, le lundi et un autre jour
qui varie. **f** Je ne suis pas souvent libre au week-end, c'est fatigant et de
temps en temps, il y a des clients désagréables. **g** Le patron est gentil,
l'ambiance est agréable et il y a des clients sympathiques qui laissent de
bons pourboires.

 avez-vous compris? (p.152)   **1** G, **2** I, **3** F, **4** A, **5** J,
6 B, **7** H, **8** E, **9** D, **10** C.

 avez-vous compris? (p.154)   The ideal candidate
must speak Spanish. English is an advantage. He / she is between 25
and 45 and has experience of word processing and spreadsheets. He /
she must be of immaculate appearance.

 avez-vous compris? (p.156)

Nom	BRUNET
Prénom	Anne-Laure
Date de naissance	10 juillet …
Situation de famille	Célibataire
Adresse	35 rue de Mulhouse, Dijon
Diplômes	Bac + 3
	BTS Commerce
Langues étrangères	Espagnol, Anglais
Expérience professionnelle	Secrétaire comptable pour Eurocor (7 ans)
	Stage de 6 mois à Madrid, Espagne.

avez-vous compris? (p.158) **1** Il a mis la main à la
pâte. **2** Il a fait beaucoup de progrès en français, surtout pour parler.
3 poursuit des études universitaires **4** Il n'a pas eu le temps de faire de
tourisme. **5** qui font la spécificité de la cuisine française **6** s'initier **7** Il a
découvert les secrets de la fabrication. **8** ont récemment accueilli **9** Il a
appris des tas de choses. **10** tous les aspects du métier

à vous! (p.159) *(Suggested answer)* J'ai passé trois
semaines dans un petit restaurant breton qui s'appelle La Boule d'Or et
dont les propriétaires sont Lucas et Gwenaëlle Le Guennec. Lucas est
aussi le cuisinier. Gwenaëlle s'occupe de la comptabilité, des achats de la
nourriture, des boissons etc. Ils ont deux employés qui travaillent à plein
temps, un jeune homme qui aide à la cuisine et une serveuse.
Pendant mon séjour j'ai participé à toutes les activités du restaurant – j'ai
mis la main à la pâte à la cuisine (j'ai appris à faire les galettes et le far),
j'ai passé des commandes par ordinateur et j'ai même servi à table, ce
qui est très fatigant. J'ai donc découvert tous les aspects du métier de
restaurateur. J'ai aussi passé deux jours dans une ferme où j'ai aidé à
faire du cidre.
Ce stage m'a beaucoup apporté à plusieurs points de vue: j'ai
découvert le monde du travail, la vie quotidienne d'un restaurant, la
culture bretonne, en particulier la gastronomie et la musique, et j'ai aussi
fait beaucoup de progrès en français. Je peux donc dire que l'expérience
a été très intéressante et très bénéfique. J'aimerais retourner dans la
région car, malheureusement, je n'ai pas eu le temps de faire
de tourisme.

EXERCICES **A 1** ennuyeux, **2** intéressant, **3** épuisant,
4 dangereux, **5** bien payé, **6** varié, **7** mal payé. **B 1** reçu, **2** candidature,
3 poste, **4** bilingue, **5** heureux, **6** curriculum vitae, **7** entretien,
8 reconnaissants, **9** rendez-vous, **10** sentiments distingués.
C Ad A 1 Salesperson. **2** Knowledge of supermarket and self-service
stores; able to sell on the telephone; knowledge of fresh foods or fruit
and vegetables. **3** Able to communicate well. **4** Basic salary +
commission, plus expenses and a car. **5** Send handwritten letter with CV
and photo to agency. **Ad B 1** Secretary. **2** Excellent shorthand and
typing, perfect spoken and written English, computer skills essential.
3 Dynamic and enthusiastic person. **4** Permanent job with prospects.
5 Send letter with CV and photo to agency who will forward.
Ad C 1 Representatives. **2** Previous experience not essential.
3 Immediately available, any age, dynamic and ambitious; immaculate
appearance, preferably car owner. **4** High commissions, possibility of
rapid promotion to executive level, training given. **5** Go to the Grand
Hotel in St Laurent du Var, on Monday 10th or Tuesday 11th February
between 9 and 12 am, or 2 and 6 pm. **D** Je m'appelle Charlotte Martin.
Je suis née le seize septembre 1980. Je suis célibataire. Il y a dix ans, je
suis allée en vacances en France mais j'y suis restée deux ans. J'ai
travaillé dans un hôtel. Je suis rentrée / revenue en Angleterre il y a sept
ans et j'ai travaillé dans une usine. Il y a six ans, j'ai travaillé comme
caissière dans un supermarché. Il y a cinq ans, j'ai trouvé du travail dans
un bureau. Il y a trois ans, j'ai fait un stage d'un an en Allemagne.
Depuis mon retour, je travaille dans un magasin de vêtements à
Londres. Je parle (le) français et (l') allemand. J'aime le contact avec les
gens. **E 1** Oui, mais il y a des avantages et des inconvénients. **2** C'est
varié et intéressant et j'aime le contact avec les gens. **3** C'est fatigant

parce que la journée de travail est longue / les heures sont longues.
4 Ça dépend et je ne suis pas toujours libre le week-end. **5** Non, ce n'est
pas très bien payé / c'est mal payé. **6** En général ils sont sympathiques,
mais de temps en temps il y en a qui sont désagréables. **7** J'aime surtout
les enfants. Je suis infirmier / infirmière.

écoutez bien! **1** médecin, **2** mécanicien / garagiste,
3 hôtesse de l'air, **4** chauffeur de taxi.

lecture **1** Three of the following: housework,
ironing, child-minding, tutoring, gardening, DIY, computing. **2** People
find what they need easily, the CESU system has tax advantages and
there are now specialist organisations to help them. **3** Luncheon
vouchers and holiday vouchers. **4** By asking for two years' experience
that can be verified, giving quality control checks, asking for training and
certificates in certain areas. **5** By sending an individual with several skills,
or a team of people. **6** Because they no longer have to rely on their own
resources for childcare. **7** It has dropped significantly. **8** No, because
they still have to pay the usual social security and income tax. **9** The
employees gain health insurance, cover for accidents at work. The job
also counts towards their retirement.

Neuvième unité

avez-vous compris? (p.167) **1** F, **2** V, **3** F, **4** F, **5** F, **6**
V, **7** V, **8** F, **9** V, **10** V.

à vous! (p.167)   **1** Pat et moi avons décidé d'aller en vacances ensemble. **2** Malheureusement on n'arrive pas à se mettre d'accord. **3** On ne veut pas aller à l'étranger. **4** On a déjà prévu un long week-end à Paris. **5** Fin août. / A la fin du mois d'août. **6** Je trouve / pense qu'il y a trop de monde l'été. **7** Oui, il vaut mieux choisir une région complètement différente. **8** Merci pour vos conseils.

avez-vous compris? (p.170)   **1** Alsace, **2** train, **3** Strasbourg, **4** voiture, **5** Colmar, **6** foire, **7** bière, **8** choucroute, **9** exercice, **10** VTT.

à vous! (p.171)   **1** Nous prendrons le train. **2** Nous irons à Strasbourg. **3** Nous verrons la cathédrale gothique, de vieilles maisons médiévales, le palais Rohan, etc. **4** Nous visiterons peut-être une brasserie. **5** Nous louerons une voiture. **6** Nous boirons du vin et de la bière. **7** Nous mangerons de la choucroute. **8** Nous ferons des randonnées. **9** (L) Moi, je pêcherai la truite. / (C) Moi, je prendrai beaucoup de photos.

avez-vous compris? (p.174)   Moi, je supporte mal la chaleur … Oui nous irons d'abord à Sélestat … Nous verrons des maisons médiévales en grès rose à Colmar … Oui, mon mari pense que l'Alsace est plus belle que la Bourgogne … S'il fait mauvais / s'il pleut, nous visiterons le musée du chemin de fer ou le musée National de l'Automobile … Mon mari trouve que le paysage du Val de Loire est moins varié que celui de la Bourgogne … Et il dit que leur vin est moins bon que le nôtre.

EXERCICES **A** **1** Bonjour, monsieur / madame. Je ne sais pas où aller en vacances à Pâques. **2** Je veux rester en France. **3** Je ne suis pas très sportif / sportive et je déteste le froid. **4** Il y a trop de monde. **5** Pouvez-vous me donner des dépliants? **B** **1** irez, **2** irons, **3** pourrai, **4** visiterai, **5** verrai, **6** ferez, **7** descendrons, **8** voyagerez, **9** prendrons, **10** louerons, **11** verrez, **12** verrons, **13** verrons, **14** ferez, **15** boirai, **16** mangerai, **17** irai, **18** ferai, **19** prendrai. **C** **1** Oui, mon ami Paul et moi, on restera en Angleterre. **2** Non, on veut visiter les villes de Salisbury et Winchester. **3** On verra les belles cathédrales et de vieilles maisons, et on fera de longues promenades / randonnées. **4** Non, les hôtels coûtent trop cher. On empruntera la caravane d'un(e) ami(e). **5** Oui, après on ira au bord de la mer. **6** S'il fait beau, on se baignera et on se reposera sur la plage. **D** Je vérifierai mon passeport. J'achèterai des chèques de voyage. Je réserverai une place dans le train. Je ferai ma valise. J'emporterai un imperméable. Je descendrai dans un bon hôtel. Je réserverai une chambre avec douche et WC. Je louerai une voiture. Je visiterai les endroits historiques. Je ne perdrai pas mon temps sur la plage. Je n'irai pas au casino. Je te téléphonerai ou je t'écrirai une carte postale. **E** (*Suggested answer*) Cher Alain / Chère Aline, Nous sommes bien arrivés dans le Limousin. S'il fait beau demain, nous irons au lac de Vassivière, où nous ferons de belles promenades et nous nous baignerons. Sinon, nous ferons la visite des musées et des monuments historiques à Limoges. J'achèterai peut-être de la porcelaine! Amicalement, ____

écoutez bien! **1** Bretagne, **2** villa, **3** endroit, **4** plage, **5** soleil, **6** boules, **7** ballon, **8** sport, **9** voile, **10** cheval, **11** pêche, **12** restaurant, **13** poissons, **14** crêpes, **15** cidre, **16** costumes.

lecture   **A La bicyclette gourmande** is a trip combining good food and the comfort of a three star hotel with a cycling holiday exploring Alsace. Luggage is taken care of, and the à la carte formula includes the hire of bikes and a guide. Prices start at 580 € per person for two and a half days for a group of four.   **B** The hotel **L'Anse Colas** is just five minutes from the centre of Fort-de-France. It has a large swimming pool in the middle of a tropical garden. All the rooms are air-conditioned, have telephones, television and a large terrace with a view over the sea and the pool. The bar has a pleasant atmosphere and those with fine taste buds will appreciate the Créole and French cuisine, particularly the quail stuffed with lobster and the baked black pudding. The hotel also has a boat of 18 metres available for day cruises.

Faites le point! (unités 7–9)

1 Hier, je me suis réveillé(e) à sept heures et je me suis levé(e) cinq minutes plus tard. J'ai pris mon petit déjeuner, puis je me suis lavé(e) et je me suis habillé(e). Je suis allé(e) au travail en bus. Le midi, j'ai mangé un sandwich au café du coin avec des collègues. J'ai quitté le bureau à six heures mais je ne suis pas rentré(e) directement à la maison. Je suis allé(e) au supermarché et j'ai acheté à manger pour le dîner. Le soir, je ne suis pas sorti(e), je suis resté(e) à la maison. Après avoir fait la vaisselle, j'ai lu le journal et jai regardé la télévision. Je me suis couché(e) vers onze heures. J'ai pris un bain avant de me coucher.

2 sont allés, se sont réveillés, se sont levés, sont montés, a lu, s'est endormi, s'est réveillé, sont descendus, sont allés, s'est mis, ont repris, sont rentrés. **3 a** Serious gardener seeks job, garden maintenance, tree pruning, designing, putting in order, **b** Team of builders seeking construction work, villa, swimming pool, fencing, tiling, extension, renovation, painting, wallpapering, etc., **c** Young English waiter (19, French-speaking) seeks work in a pub, bar, café, disco, **d** Lady of 60 with own transport seeks job as a companion, housework, ironing, cooking, etc., **e** Cook wanted, good sauce maker, knowing how to make pastry.

4 Par un beau matin ensoleillé, Paul et Angélique ont décidé d'aller faire un petit tour en **moto**. Ils sont **partis** vers neuf heures du matin. Une heure plus **tard**, la moto est tombée en panne. Paul a essayé de la **réparer**. Tout à coup, il a commencé à pleuvoir. Angélique n'était **pas** contente / était **furieuse** / **en colère** et ils **se** sont **disputés**. Paul n'a pas **pu** réparer la moto et finalement, ils ont **décidé** d'aller chercher de l'aide. Ils ont **marché** longtemps à travers champs. Ils ont même **traversé** une petite rivière. Enfin, ils sont arrivés dans **un petit village pittoresque**. Ils se sont tout de suite **rendus** au garage où ils ont **trouvé** un mécanicien très sympa. Ensuite, ils ont **mangé** / **acheté** un croque-monsieur et ils ont **bu** une bière au café du village. **5 1** iront, **2** passera, **3** descendront, **4** feront, **5** fera, **6** se baignera, **7** jouera, **8** essaiera, **9** joueront, **10** feront, **11** prendra, **12** ira, **13** se reposeront, **14** verront, **15** admirera, **16** goûteront, **17** boiront, **18** manqueront, **19** auront, **20** enverront. **6** a(iv), b(ii), c(v), d(i), e(iii). **7** Demain, je me réveillerai à 7 heures et je me lèverai 5 minutes plus tard. Je prendrai mon petit déjeuner, puis je me laverai et je m'habillerai. J'irai au travail en bus. Le midi, je mangerai un sandwich au café du coin avec des collègues. Je quitterai le bureau à 6 heures, mais je ne rentrerai pas directement à la maison. J'irai au supermarché et j'achèterai à manger pour le dîner. Le soir, je ne sortirai pas, je resterai à la maison. Après avoir fait la vaisselle, je lirai le journal et je regarderai la télévision. Je me coucherai vers 11 heures. Je prendrai un bain avant de me coucher.

Dixième unité

avez-vous compris? (p.186)   **1** Non, il fera mauvais pour la saison. **2** Il y aura du verglas. **3** Le brouillard. **4** Non, il y aura de belles éclaircies. **5** Oui, il soufflera en rafales. **6** Il fera beau. **7** Non, il y aura des orages violents et beaucoup de pluie avec des risques d'inondations. **8** Non, elles seront inférieures aux moyennes saisonnières.

à vous! (p.186)   **1: Beau temps:** éclaircie, soleil, beau, ensoleillé, brise, clair, se dissiper, estival, doux, bleu. **Mauvais temps:** gris, pluvieux, orage, vent, brouillard, froid, verglas, éclair, nuageux, neige, rafale, tempête, gelée, variable, couvert, averse, alerte orange.
2: 1 pluies, **2** couvert, **3** nuages, **4** matinée, **5** ciel, **6** averses, **7** rafales, **8** brouillards, **9** soleil, **10** vents, **11** moyennes, **12** orages, **13** inondations, **14** ensoleillé, **15** éclaircies.

avez-vous compris? (p.189)   **1** Elle a déménagé. **2** Non, Laurent l'aidera. **3** Il achètera des pinceaux, un rouleau et de la colle. **4** Du papier à rayures pour le séjour, du papier à fleurs pour sa chambre. **5** Ils commenceront le week-end de la Pentecôte. **6** Ils mettront des journaux par terre. **7** Non, ils peindront le plafond avant de coller le papier peint. **8** Elle devra changer les rideaux et les coussins. **9** Ils iront dans une autre maison. / Ils déménageront.

☞ **à vous!** (p.189) **1** le plafond, **2** le mur, **3** la moquette, **4** le rideau, **5** le journal / le magazine, **6** l'escabeau, **7** le pot de peinture / la peinture, **8** le papier peint, **9** le rouleau, **10** le pinceau.

💡 **avez-vous compris?** (p.191) **1** G, **2** F, **3** J, **4** I, **5** B, **6** L, **7** H, **8** C, **9** E, **10** A, **11** D, **12** K.

☞ **à vous!** (p.191) Chauffage **10**, Créativité **8**, **11**, Décoration **4**, **12**, Electricité **2**, **7**, Jardin **1**, **2**, **16**, Luminaire **6**, Maçonnerie **13**, **17**, Menuiserie **9**, **17**, Plomberie **3**, **5**, **18**, Quincaillerie **14**, **15**.

💡 **avez-vous compris?** (p.192) **1** Elle veut mettre une étagère dans sa cuisine. **2** Elle y rangera ses livres de recettes. **3** Parce que cela coûtera moins cher. **4** *Suggested answer*. Elle aura besoin de bois, d'une scie, d'un rabot, d'un marteau, de clous, de pinceaux et de peinture. **5** Son père. **6** Un mètre, une scie et un rabot. **7** Elle a décidé de l'acheter en ligne / sur internet. **8** *2 out of the following:* Parce que l'étagère est jolie, parce qu'elle ne coûte pas cher, parce que Chantal ne devra pas la faire elle-même.

☞ **à vous!** (p.193) **1** Portant, **2** Entendant, **3** Tenant, **4** tremblant, **5** Sortant, **6** Sachant, **7** Ayant, **8** courant.

EXERCICES **A** **1** irons, **2** prendrons, **3** préféreront, **4** arriverons, **5** louerons, **6** partirons, **7** descendrons, **8** passerons, **9** fera, **10** joueront, **11** amuserons, **12** verrons, **13** auront, **14** achèteront. **B** **1** Non, je resterai à la maison et je referai les peintures. **2** Non, ma femme achètera des pinceaux, de la colle et des rouleaux. **3** Merci, elle a déjà choisi la peinture et le papier peint. **4** Non, malheureusement. Jacques et Patricia feront de la voile et Sylviane sortira avec son petit ami. **5** Naturellement, elle lavera les murs et le plafond. **6** Moi, je peindrai le plafond et je collerai le papier peint. **7** J'espère (bien / que oui)!

C **Arlette** lira, elle écoutera de la musique et elle regardera la télévision de temps en temps. Elle tricotera un peu ou elle fera du crochet. Elle téléphonera régulièrement à ses amies. **Jeanne** ira au concert et au théâtre. Elle ira dans les grands magasins et elle achètera beaucoup de vêtements. Pour garder la ligne, elle fera de la musculation ou de l'aérobic. Elle sortira beaucoup avec ses amis et ils iront souvent au restaurant. **Julien** jouera aux cartes et aux échecs. Il jouera aussi du piano et de la guitare. Il fera de la natation et de l'équitation. Il lira beaucoup et il invitera des amis chez lui. Il ira quelquefois au stade. **Jean-Paul** jouera au golf et aux boules. Il fera du jogging le matin. Il ira au marché où il achètera beaucoup de fruits et de légumes. À la maison il fera du bricolage ou du jardinage. **D** **1** D, **2** E, **3** H, **4** F, **5** G, **6** A, **7** B, **8** C. **E** **1** pleut, **2** prendra, **3** sortirons, **4** mettrons, **5** sera, **6** dînera, **7** offre, **8** enverrai, **9** commanderai, **10** arriverai, **11** iront, **12** descendront. **F** (*Suggested answer*) Chère Sylvie, Cette année, nous avons décidé de partir en vacances au mois de juin, pour éviter les embouteillages. Nous irons d'abord en Vendée, car c'est une région de votre pays que nous ne connaissons pas tellement bien. Nous passerons huit jours sur la côte où nous nous reposerons. Nous nous baignerons, nous ferons de belles promenades en bateau et nous passerons l'après-midi sur la plage. S'il fait vraiment trop chaud, on achètera un parasol – de nos jours il faut faire attention au soleil, n'est-ce pas? Le soir nous irons au restaurant où nous goûterons aux spécialités de la région, du poisson et des fruits de mer. Ensuite nous irons dans les Pyrénées où nous avons loué un petit chalet. Nous ferons souvent de longues randonnées à pied. Nous espérons voir beaucoup d'animaux et de fleurs sauvages, même des espèces rares. Frank ira quelquefois à la pêche. Moi, je compte faire quelques tableaux pendant les vacances, s'il y a assez de place dans le coffre pour toutes mes affaires! Et vous Sylvia? Pensez-vous toujours aller aux États-Unis? Écrivez-moi pour me raconter vos projets de vacances. Amicalement, Anne.

Cher Henri, J'étais très content de recevoir de tes nouvelles, et de savoir que tu vas mieux maintenant. Je t'écris pour t'inviter à passer quelques jours chez moi. J'ai des vacances à prendre à la fin du mois, et je serai très content de te revoir. Nous pourrons d'abord aller à Londres, où nous visiterons les musées à South Kensington ou la tour de Londres, que tu n'as pas encore vue. Le soir nous irons au théâtre pour voir une nouvelle pièce, ou au restaurant pour manger des spécialités anglaises comme le rosbif. Si tu es trop fatigué nous rentrerons tôt, nous prendrons un petit repas chez nous, et nous boirons de la bière anglaise que tu aimes tant! Si tu en as envie, nous pourrons visiter des châteaux célèbres aux environs de Londres, par exemple le château de Windsor ou le palais de Hampton Court. Mais si tu préfères rester à la maison nous pourrons bavarder et bricoler un peu! En espérant te revoir bientôt, Bien amicalement, Albert.

écoutez bien!   **Première partie**   **1** Because of the weather; there will be showers everywhere. **2** In Brittany. **3** In the mountains, above 2000 metres. **4** Very cool on the coast. **5** North north-

west. **6** Because the weather will improve. **7** On the Atlantic coast.
8 Sunny. **9** Between 12° and 16°C. **10** Between 16° and 19°C.
Deuxième partie Woman 3, 9, **Young girl** 1, 4, 5, 8. **Man** 2, 6, 7, 10.
The woman is going to Normandy, because she is from that region. She
is staying for a week in a hotel. The young girl is going to Corsica because
she likes the idea and she loves the sea and sun. She will spend five or
six weeks camping or sleeping in the open air on the beach. The man will
stay at home because his wife is away. He will be free for a month.

lecture **1** The first to Hugo's daughter, the second
to Baudelaire's lover. **2** He mentions **l'aube** at the beginning and then
l'or du soir in the final stanza. **3** He says: **je marcherai les yeux fixés
sur mes pensées, sans rien voir au-dehors, sans entendre aucun
bruit**; also **Je ne regarderai ni l'or du soir qui tombe, ni les
voiles,** i.e. not seeing nor hearing anything around him. **4** Probably to a
real or imaginary sunset. **5 chaleurs, flambeaux, doubles lumières,
flamme, éclair. 6 1: demain, je partirai, j'irai, je marcherai, je ne
regarderai, quand j'arriverai, je mettrai. 2: nous aurons, deux
cœurs seront, réfléchiront, échangerons, plus tard un Ange
…viendra ranimer. 7 1: blanchit, l'or, le houx vert 2: rose, bleu.
8 je sais que tu m'attends, Je ne puis demeurer loin de toi plus
longtemps. 9** The last stanza: **Et plus tard un Ange entr'ouvrant
les portes …**

Onzième unité

 avez-vous compris? (p.200) **1** Il n'est plus au chômage. Il a retrouvé du travail. **2** Représentant. **3** Bien payé, avec commissions. Une voiture de service et cinq semaines de vacances. **4** Une société de fournitures de bureau. **5** Non, il n'a pas pris de vacances. **6** Il modernise les bureaux de Boulogne. **7** Il sera livré rapidement et Déveine lui fera une remise si la commande est importante. **8** Le mardi de la semaine suivante.

avez-vous compris? (p.202) **1** M. Lachance. **2** M. Lachance. **3** M. Déveine. **4** Les deux. **5** M. Lachance. **6** M. Lachance. **7** M. Déveine. **8** M. Lachance. **9** M. Lachance. **10** M. Déveine. **11** Les deux. **12** Les deux. **13** M. Déveine. **14** M. Lachance. **15** M. Déveine.

à vous! (p.202) **1** Managing Director: M. Lachance, **2** Personal Assistant: Mme Manès, **3** Chief accountant: M. Blanchet, **4** Commercial Manager: M. Balland, **5** Advertising Manager: Mlle Amandin, **6** Marketing Manager: M. Pinot, **7** Sales Manager: M. Masset, **8** Purchasing Manager: Mme Jolivel, **9** Human Resources Manager: Mme Chevrinais, **10** Reps: Mlle Abadi, M. Stavalen, **11** Secretaries: Mlle Paynot, Mme Rieux, Mme Viard, **12** Computer operator: Mlle Nicot, **13** Receptionist: Mme Lacroix, **14** Switchboard Operator: Mlle Flon.

avez-vous compris? (p.204)   **1** secrétaire de direction,
2 entreprise, **3** s'appelle, **4** poste 174, **5** Monsieur Durant, **6** rendez-vous, **7** le plus tôt possible, **8** semaine, **9** libre, **10** le mercredi,
11 11 heures, **12** convient.

avez-vous compris? (p.206)   **1** vrai, **2** vrai, **3** faux,
4 vrai, **5** vrai, **6** faux, **7** vrai, **8** faux, **9** vrai, **10** vrai, **11** faux, **12** vrai.

à vous! (p.207)   6 – 10 – 4 – 8 – 1 – 9 – 2 – 5 – 7 – 3.

avez-vous compris? (p.208)   **1** On vérifie les robinets,
le gaz, on éteint les cigarettes et on ferme la porte à clef. **2** Une tentative
de cambriolage, une fuite de gaz, un début d'incendie ou une
inondation. **3** Oui, parce que c'est un service permanent et rapide.

à vous! (p.208)   **1** Fuite de gaz fatale, **2** Voisin courageux
évite cambriolage, **3** Météo – Des Inondations en Normandie,
4 Sans-abri après le terrible incendie.

avez-vous compris? (p.210)   **1** F, **2** F, **3** V, **4** V, **5** F,
6 F, **7** F, **8** V, **9** V, **10** F, **11** F, **12** V.

à vous! (p.211)   **1** entreprise, **2** créée, **3** collègue, **4** cent,
5 acheter, **6** vendre, **7** frais, **8** poids, **9** arêtes, **10** date limite de
consommation, **11** pays, **12** clients, **13** visite, **14** téléphoner, **15**
ordinateur, **16** inconvénient, **17** vacances, **18** administration.

EXERCICES   **A** **1** chômage, **2** retrouver, **3** rémunéré/payé, **4** service, **5** d'occasion, **6** semaines, **7** an, **8** bureau, **9** remise, **10** commande, **11** société / firme, **12** succursales, **13** déplacement, **14** recruter, **15** annonces.   **B** (*Suggested answer*) Chère Marie-Claude, Comment vas-tu? Moi, ça va très bien, surtout depuis que j'ai changé de travail. Je suis maintenant opérateur informatique pour une société multinationale qui s'appelle Eurocor. J'ai maintenant un bon salaire et six semaines de vacances par an mais je n'ai pas de voiture de service. Le travail est très intéressant et mes collègues sont sympathiques. Malheureusement, le patron est souvent de mauvaise humeur. Heureusement qu'il va souvent à l'étranger! Mon bureau se trouve dans le centre-ville et je peux y aller en bus. C'est seulement à une demi-heure de chez moi. Maintenant que je ne travaille plus le week-end, tu dois venir me voir. Donne-moi un coup de fil pour fixer une date. À très bientôt. Amicalement, Émile   **C** **1** Je voudrais le poste 218, s'il vous plaît. **2** Je voudrais parler à Madame Monnet. **3** Je n'ai pas reçu votre catalogue et vos échantillons. **4** Je suis / Je m'appelle … **5** J'habite … **6** Vous faites des remises sur les commandes importantes? **7** Est-ce que vous livrez rapidement? **8** Merci beaucoup, monsieur. Au revoir.

D (*Suggested answer*)

GIGANTESQUE EXPLOSION ÉVITÉE DE JUSTESSE GRACE À UN CHEF DES VENTES ATTENTIF

Ce matin-là Paul Mercier, chef des ventes d'une petite entreprise de banlieue, est arrivé au bureau de bonne heure pour finir un rapport urgent pour un client important. Il a retiré sa veste et il s'est mis au travail sans délai.

<u>Peu de temps après</u>, il a senti une drôle d'odeur. Il a levé la tête et a regardé par la fenêtre. <u>A sa grande surprise</u>, il a vu de la fumée noire sortir de l'usine de produits chimiques en face de son bureau.

Il a <u>tout de suite</u> téléphoné aux sapeurs-pompiers. Il a expliqué que l'incendie était particulièrement dangereux à cause du risque d'explosion. Les pompiers ont <u>immédiatement</u> quitté la caserne. Il y avait beaucoup de circulation et leur voiture a avancé assez lentement malgré la sirène.

<u>Sans perdre de temps</u>, les pompiers ont évacué les locataires de l'immeuble voisin. Quand les gens ont vu qu'un homme était coincé au deuxième étage du bâtiment, l'un des pompiers est monté <u>sur-le-champ</u> à l'échelle.

<u>En arrivant</u>, il a calmé l'homme qui paniquait et il l'a aidé à descendre <u>sans attendre</u>.

Les pompiers ont réussi à éteindre l'incendie <u>environ deux heures plus tard</u>. Il n'y a pas eu d'explosion et personne n'a été <u>grièvement</u> blessé ni brûlé. L'homme, qui était <u>en fait</u> le directeur de l'usine, a serré la main à Paul pour le remercier et lui exprimer sa reconnaissance. Il lui a dit: 'Non seulement vous m'avez sauvé la vie et la vie de mes employés, mais grâce à vous, l'usine n'est pas <u>totalement</u> détruite et les ouvriers ne seront pas au chômage.'

écoutez bien!   **1** Mr Lapoix would like to meet the Sales manager. He will be in Paris on 11 and 12 May and wants to know if he could call then. His telephone number is 02.51.16.35.67 and his e-mail: lapoix@aol.com (13.48). **2** Miss Duval, Mrs Dumas' secretary, has a message for the General Manager. Mrs Dumas is sorry but she will arrive on April 18th, not 16th as arranged. (14.05) **3** Mr Tanguy has not received the catalogue requested a month ago and wants another sent,

ASAP, to Société Meublot et Fils, 72 boulevard de la Résistance in
Chartres, post code: 28005. (14.17) **4** Mrs Aubry would like some details
about article HK628. Please call her back on 02.96.58.15.44, ASAP. (14.36)

Douzième unité

avez-vous compris? (p.216)   **1** les clients d'un café,
2 des badauds, **3** un chien, **4** les musiciens / le groupe 'MiDoRé',
5 un estivant, **6** des enfants, **7** un serveur / une serveuse / un garçon de
café, **8** des seniors, **9** des amis, **10** un cycliste.

à vous! (p.216)   **Dans la rue:** Il faisait beau. Tous les gens
portaient des vêtements d'été. Il y avait beaucoup de circulation car il
était déjà six heures. Quelques piétons marchaient d'un pas pressé pour
rentrer chez eux mais les badauds regardaient les vitrines des magasins.
Une dame promenait son chien. Trois personnes attendaient l'autobus. Il
y avait du monde aux terrasses des cafés où les clients prenaient des
boissons rafraîchissantes ou mangeaient des glaces. Un monsieur sortait
de la boulangerie une baguette à la main. Des jeunes faisaient la queue
devant le cinéma pour voir le dernier Tarantino. Et moi, je t'attendais
depuis une heure!

avez-vous compris? (p.218)   **1** Dans un petit village
de montagne. **2** La neige. **3** Oui, elle a eu une jeunesse très agréable.
4 Non, elle a travaillé tout de suite après son bac. **5** Pour gagner sa vie /
de l'argent. **6** Non, elle partageait un petit appartement avec des

copines. **7** Elle achetait des vêtements, des disques, des livres et allait en vacances à l'étranger. **8** Elle sortait presque tous les soirs. **9** Elle ne regardait pas la télévision. / Elle n'avait pas de téléviseur. **10** Non, parce qu'elle est épuisée et qu'elle s'endort devant.

👉 **à vous!** (p.218) (*Suggested answer*) 1d, 2g, 3b, 4h, 5f, 6c, 7e, 8a.

💡 **avez-vous compris?** (p.220) **1** Liliane, **2** Liliane, **3** Lililane, **4** Marielle, **5** Marielle, **6** Les deux, **7** Liliane, **8** Marielle, Liliane, **10** Les deux, **11** Marielle, **12** Liliane.

💡 **avez-vous compris?** (p.223) **1** Yvon, **2** Jojo, **3** Noémie et Farida, **4** Erwan, **5** Jules et Tamalou2, **6** Noémie, **7** Lulu, **8** Yvon et Aviofobik, **9** Erwan, **10** Jojo, **11** Aviofobik, **12** Aviofobik, Farida, Jules et Erwan, **13** Jojo, **14** Tamalou2, **15** Jules, **16** Linda.

💡 **avez-vous compris?** (p.225) **1** Noémie a dit que les familles nombreuses bénéficiaient de réductions sur les billets de train. **2** Linda a dit qu'elle avait payé une amende parce qu'elle n'avait pas composté son billet.

👉 **à vous!** (p.225) Ecologix a dit qu'en regardant autour de lui / d'elle, il / elle constatait que l'énorme majorité des cyclistes, ceux qui roulaient pour le plaisir, n'utilisaient jamais le vélo comme moyen de transport (pour aller bosser, déplacements utiles quotidiens etc ...). Il / elle posait donc la question: 'Faites-vous des kms utiles à vélo?'

Maillojaun a dit il n'y avait pas beaucoup de cyclistes sur ce forum, qu'il
y avait surtout des gens qui regardaient les vélos à la télé. Pour sa part
il / elle ne roulait pas le dimanche en club mais il / elle allait travailler
tous les jours à vélo (20 km aller-retour) que ça lui avait fait faire des
économies incroyables (essence, assurance voiture, entretien etc ...) :
qu'il / elle n'avait plus de 2ème voiture.

SystemD a dit qu'il / elle faisait environ 100km A/R par jour au printemp
et en été pour se rendre à l'école, que ça lui permettait d'avoir un bon
entraînement ... Mais que pour le plaisir il / elle jouait au tennis et
qu'il / elle faisait du taekwondo, que ça le / la changeait.

Super Nana a dit que si, sur ce forum il y avait des gens qui faisaient du
vélo, qu'elle sortait en club tous les dimanches, qu'elle regardait aussi le
cyclisme à la tv, qu'elle utilisait plutôt le vélo que la voiture pour aller
chercher son pain à 500m et que de toutes façons, vu le prix de
l'essence, il fallait économiser.

EXERCICES

A 1 The previous year on 12 June. **2** Four
hours, from 8 to 12 pm. **3** It went up by 15%. **4** To the fact that people
couldn't watch television. **1** Il regardait la télévision. **2** Elle se lavait les
cheveux. **3** Elle prenait un bain. **4** Elle bavardait. **5** Il était au cabaret.
6 Ils écrivaient des cartes postales. **7** Ils étaient au restaurant /
mangeaient / dînaient. **8** Ils se promenaient. **9** Il fumait la pipe. **10** Elle
lisait le journal. **B 1** étais, **2** travaillais, **3** trouvaient, **4** était, **5** avais,
6 parlais, **7** était, **8** habitais, **9** restais, **10** sortais, **11** allions, **12** mangions,
13 visitais, **14** faisais, **15** pouvais, **16** avais, **17** était, **18** manquait.
C Use EXERCICE B as a model. **D** Sylvie a dit qu'elle n'était pas née à
Grasse mais qu'elle y habitait depuis quinze ans maintenant. Qu'elle

aimait beaucoup cette région. Qu'elle travaillait dans une usine de parfum. Qu'elle commençait à huit heures du matin. Que le midi les employés avaient deux heures pour déjeuner et que quand il faisait beau, elle allait à la plage avec des collègues. Qu'ils se baignaient et mangeaient des sandwichs. Que le soir, elle finissait à six heures et demie. Que l'hiver, elle rentrait directement chez elle et qu'elle regardait la télévision, mais que l'été elle sortait presque tous les soirs.

écoutez bien!   **À la plage 1** faux, **2** vrai, **3** faux, **4** faux, **5** vrai, **6** vrai, **7** vrai, **8** faux, **9** vrai, **10** vrai, **11** faux, **12** faux.

lecture   **À la Martinique 1** In a hotel in Sainte-Anne, which is on the southern coast of the island. **2** He used to get up early and go for a swim before breakfast. **3** Because the beach was deserted and quiet and he loved to listen to the sea. **4** It was a beautiful white sandy beach lined with coconut trees. **5** He went back to the beach to swim and sunbathe. **6** Of an indescribable blue and usually cloudless. **7** At the hotel. **8** Fish or shellfish dishes. **9** Pineapples because he loves them and they are plentiful in Martinique, and bananas because they melted in your mouth like honey. **10** No, he visited other parts of the island. **11** The island of Dominica. **12** The volcanic eruption of Mont Pelée destroyed the town of Saint-Pierre and surrounding villages. **13** The Pagerie museum dedicated to Josephine who was to become empress of France, the rum distillery in Gros Morne and Fort-de-France, the capital city. **14** He used to paint and try and capture its animation and colour. **15** Yes, the sale of several of his paintings covered the cost of his holiday.

Faites le point! (unités 10–12)

1 Temps très variable avec vent de secteur **sud**-ouest modéré sur le nord du pays. Très nuageux avec **pluie** en Bretagne; **averses** aux environs de Dijon.

Sur les autres régions, le temps restera instable, les éclaircies devenant belles l'après-midi sur la côte **atlantique**, mais le ciel restera **couvert** dans l'Est. Des Pyrénées aux Alpes, **beau** temps ensoleillé, avec quelques **orages** en Corse.

Les températures minimales seront comprises entre **8** et **12** degrés sur la moitié **nord** du pays. Les maximums atteindront 14 à 17 degrés sur la moitié **sud**.

2 d, h, b, e, g, i, a, c, f. **3 a** Allô! Je voudrais parler à monsieur Delarue. **b** Je voudrais prendre rendez-vous avec lui. **c** Non, je ne suis pas libre cette semaine. **d** Oui, sauf mercredi. **e** Le quinze? / Mardi quinze? / C'est (bien) le quinze? **f** Mardi matin, ça va / c'est possible. **g** Très bien / Parfait. **h** Monsieur / Madame / Mademoiselle … **4 a** Allô, Dupont Frères, j'écoute! **b** Je regrette / Je suis désolé(e), la ligne est occupée. Vous voulez / Voulez-vous attendre? **c** Bien sûr / Naturellement. Pouvez-vous me donner vos coordonées? **d** Ça s'écrit comment? / Pouvez-vous épeler, s'il vous plaît? **e** Merci. Et quel est le numéro de téléphone? **f** Très bien. Je lui ferai la commission. **g** Oui. C'est robert point dupont arobase ola point com. **5 a** étais, **b** allais, **c** avaient, **d** passions, **e** était, **f** avait, **g** faisions, **h** jouions, **i** faisions, **j** avaient, **k** s'appelait, **l** aimait.

Treizième unité

avez-vous compris? (p.237) **1** Mademoiselle Persiaux.
2 De Reims. **3** Bibliothécaire. **4** L'Everest. **5** Dans les Alpes. **6** L'océan
Pacifique. **7** 56 mètres. **8** En Suisse. **9** Le désert du Sahara. **10** 18 degrés.

à vous! (p.237) **1** plus, **2** plus, **3** moins, **4** moins,
5 moins, **6** aussi.

avez-vous compris? (p.239) **1** vrai, **2** vrai, **3** faux,
4 faux, **5** vrai, **6** vrai, **7** faux, **8** faux, **9** vrai, **10** vrai.

à vous! (p.239) (*Suggested answer*) Le Luxembourg est
plus petit que la Belgique. La Belgique est plus peuplée que la Suisse. La
Suisse est moins grande que la France. La Belgique n'est pas aussi
grande que la Suisse. La Côte-d'Ivoire a plus d'habitants que la Belgique.
Le Québec est aussi peuplé que la Suisse. La France est plus grande que
la Côte-d'Ivoire. Le Québec est plus grand que la France.

avez-vous compris? (p.241) **1** sombre, gris, morne,
l'ensemble manquait de couleur, **2** les couleurs sont aussi moins vives
qu'en Martinique, c'est très différent, **3** ouverts, bruyants, animés,
4 impressionnants, anciens, il y en a tellement, magnifique, imposante,
5 excellente, variée, pour tous les goûts, **6** plus varié, sur une plus
grande échelle, trois fois plus haut.

à vous! (p.241) (*Suggested answers*) **1** Un éléphant est plus lourd qu'un crocodile. Un serpent est aussi dangereux qu'un crocodile. **2** Un bonbon est plus sucré qu'une pomme. Une pomme est moins juteuse qu'un ananas. **3** Un yaourt est aussi bon qu'une carotte pour la santé et pour la ligne. Un yaourt a moins de calories qu'une glace. **4** Un canal est plus droit qu'une rivière. Une rivière est moins grande qu'un fleuve. **5** Un vélo coûte moins cher qu'une voiture. Un avion est plus rapide qu'une voiture. **6** Au travail, un ordinateur est plus utile qu'un téléviseur. Un téléphone est meilleur marché qu'un téléviseur.

avez-vous compris? (p.243) **1** J, **2** J, **3** J, **4** E, **5**, **6** J, **7** E, **8** E, **9** E, **10** E, **11** J, **12** E.

avez-vous compris? (p.245) **1** Annette. **2** Parce qu'elle est plus studieuse. **3** Parce qu'il sort souvent et fait beaucoup de sport. **4** Au collège, c'est lui qui court le plus vite et qui saute le plus haut. **5** Il s'entraîne régulièrement. **6** La danse et la gymnastique. **7** Parce qu'elle n'aime pas la compétition. **8** Non, mais elle fait du yoga. **9** Parce qu'elle ne peut pas parler. **10** Elle compose ses menus. **11** Si!, **12** Oui, **13** Si!, **14** Si!, **15** Non, **16** Oui, **17** Si!, **18** Non.

à vous! (p.246) (*Suggested answer*) Un cascadeur fait le métier le plus dangereux. Un ouvrier est le moins bien payé. Faire du sport est le passe-temps le plus sain. Regarder la télévision est l'occupation la moins utile. Les chiens sont les meilleurs compagnons de l'homme. Les dauphins sont les animaux les plus fascinants. La jeep est le véhicule le plus pratique dans le désert. Le métro est le transport en commun le plus rapide en ville.

avez-vous compris? (p.247)   **1** faux, **2** vrai, **3** vrai, **4** vrai, **5** faux, **6** faux, **7** faux, **8** vrai.

à vous! (p.247)   **1** valise, **2** enfants, **3** maison, **4** lunettes, **5** voiture, **6** sac, **7** robe, **8** dessin.

EXERCICES   **A** (*Suggested answer*) Les cheveux de Catherine sont plus longs que ceux de Paule. Nadine a les cheveux les plus courts. Nadine est plus mince et plus jeune que Catherine. Paule est plus âgée que Nadine et Catherine. Elle est la plus grosse. Elle a les pieds les plus grands et elle porte les chaussures les plus lourdes. La jupe de Catherine est plus longue que celle de Nadine. La veste de Nadine est plus courte que celle de Catherine. Les boucles d'oreille de Nadine sont plus grandes que celles de Catherine. Paule porte les vêtements les moins élégants. Catherine est plus jolie que Paule, mais Nadine est la plus jolie. **B** **1** La Martinique est moins grande que la Guadeloupe. **2** La Guadeloupe est moins peuplée que la Martinique. **3** Il y a plus d'habitants à Fort-de-France qu'à Pointe-à-Pitre. **4** La Martinique est plus près de l'équateur que la Guadeloupe. **5** Il fait aussi chaud à la Guadeloupe qu'à la Martinique. **6** La Guadeloupe produit plus de sucre que la Martinique. **7** La Guadeloupe exporte moins de bananes que la Martinique. **8** La Montagne Pelée est moins haute que La Soufrière. **C** (*Suggested answer*) Mons fils est le plus intelligent de sa classe. Il a les meilleurs résultats. C'est aussi le meilleur athlète de son collège. C'est lui qui court le plus vite et qui saute le plus haut et le plus loin. À la maison, c'est lui qui m'aide le plus souvent. Il passe l'aspirateur, il met la table et il range la vaisselle. C'est lui qui lit le plus et

qui regarde le moins la télévision. Il est aussi le plus beau. Il me
ressemble!

 écoutez bien!

	LA GUYANE FRANÇAISE	MADAGASCAR
Superficie	91 000 km²	587 000 km²
Altitude maximum	Montagne Tabulaire: 830 m	Amboro: 2876 m
Population totale	200 000	18 000 000
Population de la plus grande ville	Cayenne: 60 000	Antananarivo: 1 000 000
Latitude	5 Nord	20 Sud
Longitude	53 Ouest	45 Est

Quatorzième unité

avez-vous compris? (p.253) Pauvre Jeanne! Elle est
arrivée pâle et tremblante au **collège** ce matin. Je lui ai suggéré de
s'asseoir avant de me raconter ce qui lui était arrivé. Il paraît qu'elle
venait de quitter **la station-service**, et qu'elle **respectait la limite de
vitesse**. Derrière elle, il y avait **un type** dans une grosse **BMW** qui la
suivait de trop près. **Au rond-point** elle a signalé et elle a **ralenti**.
L'homme, qui était très **impatient**, a finalement décidé de la dépasser.

Malheureusement, une autre voiture qui arrivait de la **droite** ne s'est pas arrêtée. Les deux voitures se sont heurtées. Les deux **hommes** sont **descendus** et ils ont commencé à se **disputer**.

à vous! (p.254) 4, 1, 3, 2. *The odd one is* 5.

avez-vous compris? (p.256) **1** faux, **2** faux, **3** faux, **4** vrai, **5** faux, **6** faux, **7** faux, **8** vrai, **9** faux.

à vous! (p.256) 1e, 2h, 3c, 4f, 5b, 6d, 7g, 8a.

avez-vous compris? (p.259) **1** V, **2** F, **3** V, **4** F, **5** V, **6** F, **7** V, **8** V, **9** V, **10** V.

avez-vous compris? (p.261) **1** M. Lajoux, **2** Marc Lajoux, **3** les passagers du grand salon, **4** M. Hublot, **5** les Legris, **6** personne / on ne sait pas, **7** la pianiste / M. Mercier, **8** personne / on ne sait pas / tous les passagers, **9** Jeanne, **10** M. Lajoux, **11** M. Mercier, **12** personne / on ne sait pas, **13** Mme Cohen, **14** personne / on ne sait pas, **15** tous les passagers.

à vous! (p.261) **1** participais, chantais, ai quitté, **2** jouait, avait, a quitté, **3** étais, mettais, suis sortie, ai oublié, **4** faisais, buvais, ai fini / ai vidé, **5** écrivais / envoyais, me rasais, ai rangé, ai mis, **6** étions, nous sommes réveillés, **7** me faisais, me suis levée, me suis habillée, **8** regardais, ai rouspété, **9** bavardais / parlais, suis allée / me suis rendue.

avez-vous compris? (p.263) **1** un pantalon, **2** il n'aimait pas la couleur, **3** marron, **4** non, elle n'a trouvé sa taille qu'en rouge, **5** non, ils les déteste, **6** la laine lui donne des démangeaisons, et il n'aime pas la coupe, **7** il préfère être remboursé, **8** non, il l'a laissé à la maison.

avez-vous compris? (p.264) **1** vêtements, **2** couleur, **3** pantalon, **4** marron, **5** carreaux, **6** polyester, **7** pull / pull-over, **8** reçu, **9** an.

à vous! (p.265) **1** J'ai acheté cette veste récemment mais, à la lumière du jour, je n'aime pas la couleur. **2** Je voudrais la changer. Ça dépend des couleurs que vous avez. **3** Je déteste les carreaux et les rayures. **4** Je fais du –. **5** Je suis désolé(e), je l'ai oublié!

EXERCICES **A 1** quitter la station-service, **2** roulais à moins de 70 kilomètres à l'heure, **3** regardé dans mon rétroviseur avant de signaler, **4** ralenti, **5** quelqu'un me suivait de très près, **6** j'étais très patient(e), **7** je voulais tourner à droite, **8** suis reparti(e) après l'arrivée de la police. **B 1** Grand-mère fumait dans sa chambre, tante Cécile jouait aux cartes avec Colette, grand-père faisait des réparations dans la salle de bain, Jean-Pierre faisait la vaisselle dans la cuisine, le chien dormait, M. Dupré lisait, Mme Dupré passait l'aspirateur, Paul faisait ses devoirs dans le salon. **2** Grand-mère a éteint sa cigarette, tante Cécile a rangé les cartes / a mis les cartes dans le tiroir, Colette est descendue, grand-père est sorti de la salle de bain, Jean-Pierre a cassé un verre, le chien s'est réveillé, M. Dupré a fermé son livre, Mme Dupré a arrêté l'aspirateur et s'est dirigée vers le téléphone, Paul a posé son crayon / stylo et s'est levé.   **C 1** était, **2** se levait, **3** partait, **4** a perdu, **5** a pris, **6** mangeait, **7** choisissait, **8** a oublié, **9** a dû, **10** faisait, **11** sortait, **12** se promenait, **13** était, **14** a eu, **15** est rentré, **16** a attrapé, **17** a passé.   **D** 1d, 2e, 3a, 4f, 5g, 6c, 7h, 8b.

écoutez bien!   **Première partie**   Heure de l'appel: 20 h 15; Nom: Madame Claude Dupont; Numéro d'adhésion: GH 52. 33. 86; Marque, modèle et couleur du véhicule: Peugeot 206 rouge; Numéro d'immatriculation: 567 IMP 75; Situation du véhicule: Sur la N12 (nationale 12) près de Rennes / entre Rennes et Fougères.
Notes supplémentaires: Femme seule, endroit isolé, dans la forêt.
Deuxième partie   **1** ronflait / le réveil / a sonné. **2** chantait / de se taire / impolie. **3** était sous la douche / le téléphone a sonné. **4** de la pop musique / son père. **5** la cuisine / a cassé une assiette. **6** jouaient / le jardin / au bras. **Troisième partie**   Number 2.

lecture   (*Suggested answer*)

You can: listen to the motorway radio on 107.7, listen to music, have information on the region, weather and traffic, avoid traffic jams and black spots, use the emergency telephones to call breakdown, stop at the numerous service areas, stretch your legs, rest, eat and drink, go through the toll without stopping if you have subscribed to the auto toll system, sign up for the auto toll on the internet.
You must: pay to use the motorway, observe the speed limit, slow down if there are road works and in bad weather, check tyre pressures when the engine is cold, adding 0.3 for motorway driving, telephone a recognised breakdown service, preferably using the orange emergency telephones, get out of the car on the passenger side, stop every two

hours and when you are tired.

You must not: drive with worn or under inflated tyres, drive at more than 130 kilometres an hour, drive too fast, get out of the car on the driver's side, repair your vehicle or change a tyre on the hard shoulder, drive for longer than two hours at a time, drive when you are tired.

Quinzième unité

avez-vous compris? (p.273) **1** Parce que la réceptionniste a dit qu'il n'y avait pas de chambre réservée au nom de Déveine. **2** Parce qu'il y a un congrès. **3** Une seule chambre. **4** Au treizième étage. **5** Oui, c'est une chambre avec douche, WC, télévision et téléphone. **6** 102 €. **7** Jusqu'à 9 heures. **8** Il doit inviter un client important à dîner. **9** Le restaurant de l'hôtel. **10** Elle est aimable, serviable et patiente. Elle donne beaucoup de conseils et de renseignements à M. Déveine et elle propose de lui réserver une table au restaurant. **11** Pour trouver un parking / garer sa voiture.
12

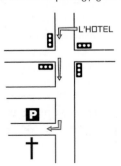

👉 **à vous!** (p.274) **1** (i) **3**, (ii) **4**, (iii) **1**, (iv) **5**, (v) **2**.
2 a complet, **b** chambre, **c** clients, **d** congrès, **e** douche, **f** restaurant,
g recommande, **h** petit déjeuner, **i** garer, **j** garage.

💡 **avez-vous compris?** (p.276) Il y avait un congrès à
l'hôtel … pour ses **affaires**. Sa chambre était au **treizième** et il y avait
beaucoup de bruit le **soir**. Les gens … parlaient fort, riaient et
chantaient parce qu'ils avaient trop **bu**. Il a passé une nuit **blanche**. …
Il a invité **un client** à dîner le **premier** soir. Le service n'était pas très
rapide parce que le personnel était **débordé**. Pourtant **le client a passé
une commande de fournitures de bureau**. Il a eu de la chance **pour
une fois**!

👉 **à vous!** (p.277) (*Suggested answers*) 1h, 2d, 3i, 4m, 5g,
6j, 7f, 8k, 9l, 10e.

💡 **avez-vous compris?** (p.279) (*Suggested answers*)
1 C'est le moyen le plus rapide pour traverser la Manche (35 minutes),
mais il faut aller à Calais qui est loin de Rouen. **2** Il faut une heure et
demie seulement, mais il faut aussi aller à Calais. **3** Très cher et moins
pratique.

👉 **à vous!** (p.280) **1** rapide, **2** facile, **3** courte, meilleur
marché, **4** liberté, **5** pire, **6** cher, pratique.

💡 **avez-vous compris?** (p.281) **1** vrai, **2** on ne sait pas,
3 vrai, **4** faux, **5** vrai, **6** faux, **7** vrai, **8** faux, **9** on ne sait pas,
10 faux.

👉 **à vous!** (p.281) La Cathédrale Notre-Dame a été reconstruite au treizième siècle après le terrible incendie de 1200. L'Église St-Maclou, qui est une ravissante construction de style gothique flamboyant, a été bâtie entre 1437, et 1517. Jeanne d'Arc a été brûlée vive sur la place du Vieux-Marché en 1431. La tourelle originelle du Beffroi a été remplacée en 1382. Le Gros-Horloge, qui était jadis dans le beffroi, a été placé dans l'arche, qui enjambe la rue, en 1527. Le palais de Justice, qui est un splendide édifice de la Renaissance, a été bâti pour abriter l'Échiquier de Normandie.

EXERCICES **A** **1** Pardon, M… pour aller à l'Hôtel de Normandie? **2** En sortant du syndicat d'initiative, je tourne à gauche. **3** Je continue tout droit jusqu'à la cathédrale et je tourne à droite. C'est loin? **4** Je traverse la place du Marché puis je prends la première à gauche. **5** Mais je cherche l'Hôtel de Normandie, pas l'Hôtel de Bretagne! **B** **1** À quelle heure servez-vous le petit déjeuner? **2** Pouvez-vous me réveiller à six heures et demie demain matin? **3** Y a-t-il un bon restaurant dans le quartier? Je dois inviter deux clients importants à dîner. **4** Je dois réserver une table? **5** Pour huit heures et demie, pour trois personnes. Il y a un garage ou un parking? **6** Où est-ce que je peux garer ma voiture? **7** C'est loin? **8** Merci, monsieur/madame. **C** Vous savez – le radium a été découvert en 1898 par Pierre et Marie Curie. Le stéthoscope a été inventé par Laënnec. Le système de lecture pour les aveugles a été créé par Louis Braille. Le tunnel sous la manche a été inauguré en 1989. Le palais de Versailles a été construit au dix-septième siècle pour le roi Louis XIV. L'arc de Triomphe a été inauguré en 1836. La Cité des sciences et de l'industrie a été créée en 1979 sur le site de l'ancien marché national de la viande à la

Villette. *La Balançoire* et *Les Baigneuses* sont des tableaux qui ont été peints par Renoir. L'opéra *Carmen* a été composé par Bizet en 1875. *Hernani* est une pièce de théâtre qui a été écrite par Victor Hugo et mise en scène en 1830. *Les Biches* est un ballet qui a été composé par Francis Poulenc et mis en scène en 1924. *La Gloire de mon père* et *Le Château de ma mère* ont été écrits par Marcel Pagnol et publiés en 1957 et 1958. **D** (*Suggested answer*) Chers Hervé et Marité, Nous sommes arrivés à Rouen samedi. Hier nous avons vu la cathédrale Notre-Dame et la place du Vieux Marché où Jeanne d'Arc a été brûlée vive. Le temps est variable et nous avons eu plusieurs averses, alors nous avons pris le Métrobus. Ce soir nous dînerons dans un petit restaurant près du Gros-Horloge. Affectueusement, –.

🎧 **écoutez bien!** **Première partie** The Tropical is ten minutes from the town centre in large gardens with tennis courts, a covered swimming pool, sauna and mini-golf. It has lifts and air-conditioning in the rooms and facilities for handicapped people. It has three restaurants, one of them self-service, and two bars, one on the terrace. There are child reductions but none for pensioners. Dogs are not allowed. **Deuxième partie** **1** The man needs a coin for his trolley. It can be obtained from the cashier's in the supermarket. **2** There are no towels in the bathroom and the bed isn't made. The chambermaid will get some towels and change the sheets. **3** The lady wants to change a dress which has shrunk. There are no more in her size, so she decides on a refund. **4** The meal is unsatisfactory because the meat is tough, the bread stale and there's a dirty fork. Unfortunately, it's the boss's day off! **5** The lady has a water leak in the kitchen. The plumber she calls is fully booked but she is given another number.

lecture (*Suggested answers*) **1** Hôtel de Lausanne, **2** Grand Hôtel de Panama, **3** Hôtel Rabelais, **4** Pacific Hôtel, **5** Hôtel de Bretagne, **6** Hôtel des Pommiers, **7** Hôtel de Brighton.

Faites le point! (unités 13–15)

1 **a** plus, **b** haute, **c** montagne, **d** profond, **e** moins, **f** chutes, chutes, **g** col, **h** grand, **i** fleuve, **j** île, **k** peuplé, **l** langue. **2** **a** les tiens, **b** les vôtres, **c** le sien, **d** les leurs, **e** la mienne / nôtre. **3** **a** réservé, **b** nuits, **c** nom, **d** douche, **e** étage, **f** coûte / fait, **g** compris, **h** supplément / plus, **i** prends, **j** clé, **k** heure, **l** désolé(e), **m** restaurant, **n** garage, **o** là / là-bas / tout de suite. **4** **a** (Vous) tournez à droite puis (vous) prenez la première à gauche. **b** (Vous) allez tout droit puis (vous) traversez la rivière / le pont. **c** (Vous) continuez jusqu'aux feux et (vous) tournez à droite. **d** (Vous) prenez la deuxième (rue) à gauche, puis (vous) tournez à droite et (vous) continuez jusqu'à l'église. **e** En sortant du parking, (vous) tournez à droite et (vous) prenez la deuxième (rue) à gauche. **f** Au rond-point (vous) tournez à gauche. **5** **a** ont décidé, **b** était, **c** sont allés, **d** se sont changés, **e** a mis, **f** a mis, **g** pleuvait, **h** ont pris, **i** était, **j** ont bien bu, **k** bien mangé, **l** étaient, **m** sont arrivés, **n** était, **o** avait, **p** se sentait, **q** sont rentrés. **6** a8, b9, c2, d7, e4, f5, g1, h10, i3, j6. **7** Cette année, Angleterre, de voyages, renseignements, intéressants, première, le ferry, contents, jour, vent, port, avant, attendre, bateau, manger, glaces, heures, vacanciers, trois, orage, vu, peur, malades, soulagement, Douvres, l'intention, l'hôtel, se reposer.

Seizième unité

avez-vous compris? (p.293) **1** endroits, **2** souvenirs, **3** cadeaux, **4** voiture, **5** excursions, **6** panoramas, **7** reposer, **8** planche à voile, **9** ski nautique, **10** pêche, **11** spécialités gastronomiques, **12** punch, **13** créole, **14** canne à sucre, **15** ananas, **16** distillerie de rhum, **17** photos, **18** villages de pêcheurs, **19** soir, **20** fous.

à vous! (p.293) **1** visiterais, **2** achèterais, **3** ferais, **4** irais, **5** pourrais, **6** essaierais, **7** boirais, **8** mangerais, **9** verrais, **10** prendrais, **11** sortirais, **12** m'amuserais.

avez-vous compris? (p.295) **1** Parce qu'il n'y a pas de neige. **2** Non, le fond de l'air est chaud / il fait chaud. **3** Ils aiment chanter. **4** Oui. Les portes des maisons sont toujours ouvertes. **5** Parce qu'il n'y a pas de sapins là-bas. **6** On se donne des cadeaux.

à vous! (p.295) 1b, 2e, 3a, 4c, 5f, 6d.

avez-vous compris? (p.297) **1** Pour la première fois de sa vie. **2** Il faisait nuit et ils n'ont rien vu. **3** Il faisait du soleil et le ciel était bleu. **4** Un immense bonhomme de neige et une bataille de boules de neige. **5** Des remontées mécaniques: des téléphériques, des tire-fesses et des télésièges. **6** La luge. **7** noires. **8** Par un accident: il est tombé.

à vous! (p.298) **1 a** (vi), **b** (viii), **c** (i), **d** (vii), **e** (ii), **f** (iii), **g** (iv), **h** (v). **2 a** snowboard, **b** à toute allure, **c** patinoire, **d** monitrice, **e** prévu.

avez-vous compris? (p.300)   a 5, b1 and 2, c4, d1, e3, f2.

à vous! (p.300)   **1** ait, **2** soit, **3** fassent, **4** aille, **5** vienne, **6** fasse.

EXERCICES   **A** Si vous veniez en Alsace … Vous visiteriez Strasbourg, la capitale, puis vous loueriez une voiture et vous descendriez jusqu'à Colmar où vous verriez de vieilles maisons typiques. Vous boiriez de la bière, vous mangeriez de la choucroute, vous pourriez même visiter une brasserie. Vous feriez des randonnées en montagne et en forêt. Vous prendriez beaucoup de photos. Vous iriez à la pêche à la truite. En un mot vous passeriez de bonnes vacances! **B** 1g, 2f, 3b, 4h, 5i, 6c, 7j, 8a, 9e, 10d. **C** Je ferais du camping, je ferais des randonnées à cheval, je mangerais des crêpes, je ferais de la voile, j'écouterais du biniou, j'écrirais des cartes postales, je jouerais au tennis, je me reposerais sur la plage – je me bronzerais au soleil et je me baignerais, je verrais des mégalithes et enfin j'irais à la pêche! **D** **1** allait, **2** voyagerait, **3** arriverait, **4** choisirait, **5** irait, **6** visiterait, **7** faisait, **8** ferait, **9** monterait, **10** était, **11** prendrait, **12** pourrait, **13** pleuvait, **14** irait, **15** assisterait. **E** **1** aille, **2** va, **3** est, **4** soit, **5** fait, **6** fasse, **7** a, **8** ait, **9** vienne, **10** vient, **11** sont, **12** soient.

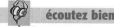 **écoutez bien!** **1** peur, colère, **2** tristesse, **3** honnêteté, **4** surprise, générosité.

lecture   There are numerous marked footpaths and about 20 routes suitable for sleigh rides. There is a special area to practise your slalom skills. You can ski off piste with specially trained guides. You can go on snowshoe outings for half a day or stay overnight in a refuge. There are also plenty of opportunities for cross-country skiing. You can experience or learn parasailing and climbing. You can play snooker and go bowling, to discos or to the cinema.

Dix-septième unité

avez-vous compris? (p.306)   **1** Madame Brède était au volant. **2** Elle voulait prendre l'autoroute. **3** Ils étaient en retard parce que Monsieur Brède ne pouvait pas se décider à choisir une cravate. **4** Non elle ne roulait pas trop vite. Elle respectait la limite de vitesse. **5** Parce que l'idiot en face d'elle avait dépassé dans le virage et qu'elle avait donné un coup de volant à droite. **6** Non, elle a son permis de conduire depuis un mois. **7** Il lui faut de l'expérience pour s'améliorer. **8** Non il n'est pas un automobiliste parfait. **9** Une fille en short a détourné son attention. **10** Tout le monde a ses moments d'inattention.

à vous! (p.307)   **1 a** écouté, **b** volant, **c** autoroute, **d** arrivé, **e** partis, **f** conduit / roulé, **g** dépassé, **h** un coup de volant, **i** dit, **j** stop, **k** arrêté **2 a** (ii), (vi), (x); **b** (i), (v), (vii); **c** (iii), (viii); **d** (iv), (ix)

avez-vous compris? (p.309) **1** le coffre, **2** les appuie-tête,
3 la clim, **4** passer les vitesses, **5** le radar de recul, **6** le régulateur de
vitesse, **7** le freinage ABS, **8** un volant réglable, **9** les airbags,
10 le GPS.

avez-vous compris? (p.311) **1** faux, **2** faux, **3** faux,
4 faux, **5** vrai, **6** faux, **7** vrai, **8** vrai, **9** faux, **10** vrai.

à vous! (p.312) **1** preniez, **2** achetiez, **3** passiez,
4 attendiez, **5** preniez.

avez-vous compris? (p.314) **1** Les étourdissements,
la toux et la pression au niveau des yeux et de la tête. **2** Du lait / Un
verre de lait. **3** Parce que c'est très ennuyeux. **4** On a faim et on a envie
d'aliments sucrés. **5** Quand on est constipé / souffre de constipation.
6 Parce qu'ils sont irritables. **7** Il faut s'étirer, respirer profondément et se
masser les tempes. **8** On peut utiliser des patchs ou des gommes
à mâcher.

à vous! (p.314) **1** effets secondaires, **2** fatigue, **3** exercice
/ activité physique, **4** excitants, **5** grignoter / manger, **6** sains,
7 constipation, **8** crus, **9** d'eau, **10** ludiques, **11** se relaxer, **12** l'envie,
13 patchs, **14** gomme, **15** médecin / tabacologue.

avez-vous compris? (p.316) **1** Alison, la
correspondante anglaise de Colette. **2** Elle a mal à la tête, elle a de la
fièvre, elle a des douleurs aiguës au ventre. **3** L'appendicite, une allergie,
une intoxication alimentaire. **4** Elle a déjà été opérée, elle n'a pas de

boutons ni de rougeurs. **5** Non, deux ou trois jours. **6** Non, seulement quelque chose pour calmer les crampes d'estomac. **7** De ne pas manger, de boire beaucoup. **8** les produits laitiers et les plats relevés.

à vous! (p.316)   1d, 2g, 3f, 4b, 5h, 6c, 7e, 8a.

avez-vous compris? (p.318)   **1** faux, **2** faux, **3** vrai, **4** vrai, **5** faux, **6** vrai, **7** vrai, **8** vrai, **9** vrai, **10** vrai.

à vous! (p.318)   **1** Derma Spray prevents and treats surface wounds that are dirty, grazes and cuts, first degree burns, insect bites. Spray 1–4 times a day. Don't apply it to broken skin with eczema or to mucous membranes. Don't spray it in your eyes. **2 a** un(e) vétérinaire, **b** un professeur, **c** un médecin, **d** un homme / une femme d'affaires, **e** un gendarme, **f** un(e) dentiste, **g** un infirmier / une infirmière / un médecin, **h** un(e) secrétaire / un(e) employé(e) de bureau, **i** un(e) employé(e) de banque, **j** un professeur / un instituteur / une institutrice / un moniteur / une monitrice.

EXERCICES   **A** 1c, 2d, 3j, 4a, 5h, 6e, 7b, 8i, 9f, 10g.
B 1 du sang, **2** du bouillon, **3** un aveugle, **4** une hanche. **C 1** Il s'appelle Rollo. **2** Vous avez raison. Il est presque aveugle parce qu'il fait du diabète. **3** Non, mais il faut qu'on lui fasse des piqûres régulières. Et votre chat? **4** Vous avez de la chance. Est-ce qu'il faut qu'il mène / Est-ce qu'il doit mener une vie calme maintenant? **5** (Moi) j'ai eu une crise cardiaque il y a trois ans. **6** Le docteur m'a dit que si j'avais pris plus d'exercice et si j'avais mangé moins de gras, je n'aurais pas été malade.

D 1 Il faut que je prenne … **2** Il faut qu'il aille … **3** Il faut que vous fassiez … **4** il ne faut pas qu'elle boive … **5** il faut que je sois … **6** il faut que vous passiez … **7** il faut qu'il vienne … **8** il ne faut pas que vous mangiez. **E** (*Suggested answer*) Ma chère Claude, C'est très gentil à toi d'écrire si tôt après notre accident. Comme tu l'auras déjà déviné, c'est moi qui étais au volant. Naturellement, ce n'était pas de ma faute. Moi, je respectais la limite de vitesse quand l'idiot d'en face a décidé de dépasser dans le virage. Résultat, j'ai donné un coup de volant à droite et malheureusement, je suis rentrée dans un arbre. Charles était furieux et nous nous sommes disputés, une fois de plus! Comme toi, je ne me sens pas bien, je suis même un peu déprimée, car j'ai des douleurs aiguës au cou. Quand je suis allée chez le médecin, il m'a dit que je devais passer une radio. En attendant, il m'a fait une ordonnance pour une crème anti-inflammatoire et des analgésiques. Rassure-toi, si je ne vais pas mieux dans deux ou trois jours je retournerai le voir. J'espère que vous passerez de bonnes vacances au Maroc – je sais que tu supportes la chaleur mieux que moi. En espérant vous revoir bientôt, Irène.

écoutez bien! **1** long, **2** en cinq minutes, **3** ans, **4** échelle, **5** cochons, **6** trois mille, **7** maladie, **8** malheur.

Dix-huitième unité

 avez-vous compris? (p.327)   **1** faux, **2** vrai, **3** faux, **4** faux, **5** faux, **6** vrai, **7** vrai, **8** faux.

 à vous! (p.327)   **1** Quelque chose … **a** d'intéressant / de stimulant, **b** de facile, **c** de sérieux / de triste, **d** de comique, **e** de cher, **f** d'ordinaire / de banal, **g** d'ordinaire / de commun, **h** de beau, **i** de sale, **j** de rapide, **k** de peu fiable / de dangereux, **l** de fatigant / d'épuisant. **2 a** jeter un coup d'œil, **b** pense, **c** crois, **d** rémédier, **e** habitue, **f** touche.

 avez-vous compris? (p.330)   **1** Pour la préparation du départ en vacances. **2** Oui, le lendemain. **3** Une grande voiture aurait coûté très cher et les chemins étaient trop mauvais. **4** Un fils. **5** Un camion pour transporter ses meubles et sa famille et la puissance d'un déménageur. **6** C'était un paysan dont la ferme était à quelques centaines de mètres de la villa. **7** Il allait deux fois par semaine vendre ses fruits au marché de Marseille. **8** Il transporterait les meubles des parents de Marcel. **9** Sa mère aurait une place sur le chariot et les autres suivraient à pied. **10** Parce que son père et son oncle avaient parlé de chasses et d'insectes.

 à vous! (p.330)   1b, 2e, 3g, 4f, 5h, 6a, 7c, 8d.

avez-vous compris? (p.332) **1** Elle laissa la porte ouverte. **2** Je ne sais pas, chuchota-t-elle. **3** Elle crut qu'il parlait dans son sommeil. **4** Un de ses yeux s'entrouvrit. **5** Elle revint dans la chambre. **6** Elle écouta d'abord. **7** Elle entendit un souffle régulier. **8** Il se retourna pesamment. **9** Elle sortit sur la pointe des pieds. **10** Elle hésita un bon moment. **11** Elle tourna le bouton avec précaution. **12** Il s'impatienta.

 à vous! (p.332) 1, 6, 4, 11, 8, 5, 3, 2, 7, 10, 9.

 avez-vous compris? (p.334) **1** emprunter, relire, **2** romans, pièces de théâtre, **3** films, **4** méridional, **5** siècle, collines, **6** soleil, **7** argent, bonheur, **8** plaisanteries, farces, **9** lecture, **10** guide, culture générale.

 à vous! (p.334) **1** *Queen Margot.* **2** *The Lacemaker.* **3** *The Umbrellas of Cherbourg.* **4** *A Man and a Woman.* **5** *And God Created Woman.* **6** *Bank Holiday.* **7** *Out of Breath.* **8** *The 400 Blows / Offences.* **9** *Tintin and the Lake of Sharks.* **10** *The 12 Labours of Astérix.* **11** *I Love You, Neither Do I.* **12** *Lift for the Scaffold.* **13** *The 101 Nights.* **14** *The Lovers of the Pont-Neuf.* **15** *The Grain of Sand.*

 avez-vous compris? (p.336) **1** François Mitterrand. **2** Non, beaucoup de Parisiens trouvaient ça choquant. **3** À la fin du dix-huitième siècle, sous Napoléon 1er. **4** Des œuvres françaises du dix-neuvième siècle. **5** Tous les gouvernements français adorent les innovations architecturales.

KEY: DIX-HUITIÈME UNITÉ 73

à vous! (p.336) Gustave Eiffel **est né** à Dijon en 1832. Il **a fini** ses études d'ingénieur en 1855, et à l'âge de 23 ans il **a commencé** sa carrière dans une compagnie de chemin de fer. Pour construire rapidement des ponts, il **a proposé** d'utiliser une structure d'acier préfabriquée. En 1861 il **a construit** à Bordeaux le premier pont métallique. Il **a construit** les écluses du canal de Panama et des usines en Égypte. Il **a bâti** le piédestal de la Statue de la Liberté qui se trouve dans la baie de New-York. Il **est devenu** riche en même temps que célèbre. Pour l'Exposition Universelle de 1889, il **a proposé** de faire construire une tour de fer de 300 mètres de haut. L'idée **a été** acceptée, mais beaucoup de Parisiens **ont protesté**. On **a envoyé** au gouvernement des pétitions demandant de raser 'cette hideuse monstruosité.' Gustave Eiffel **est mort** à Paris en 1923.

avez-vous compris? (p.338) **1** La place de la Concorde. **2** L'obélisque de Louqsor. **3** L'Opéra Garnier. **4** Le jardin des Tuileries. **5** La tour Eiffel. **6** Mac-Mahon. **7** Marie-Antoinette. **8** Le plafond de l'Opéra.

à vous! (p.339) **1** Le roi Louis XVI fut décapité place de la Concorde. **2** Les marches de l'Opéra Garnier ont 10 mètres de large. **3** L'Opéra Garnier fut dessiné par l'architecte Charles Garnier. **4** La tour Eiffel fut construite pour l'Exposition Universelle de 1889. **5** Le plafond de l'Opéra Garnier repeint par Chagall a pour thème 9 opéras et ballets célèbres / L'obélisque de Louqsor célèbre les exploits de Ramsès II. **6** La tour Eiffel joua un rôle important dans l'histoire des communications. **7** Des matériaux très coûteux, comme le marbre et l'albâtre, furent utilisés dans la construction de l'Opéra Garnier. **8** En 1792, la statue du roi Louis XV fut remplacée par une guillotine. **9** La construction de la pyramide de verre fut décidée par François Mitterrand. **10** Le musée d'Orsay fut aménagé dans une ancienne gare de Paris.

EXERCICES **A** **1** était, **2** regardèrent, **3** dit, **4** tourna, **5** ai été, **6** a ramenée, **7** faisait, **8** trouvais, **9** écoutait, **10** a trouvé.

B (*Suggested answer*) The telephone rang. It was ten o'clock. We looked at each other in surprise, then full of hope: it was Anne, she was calling to say that she had forgiven us, that she was coming back. My father leapt towards the phone, shouted 'Hello' cheerfully.

Then he only said, 'Yes, yes! Where? Yes,' almost inaudibly. I too got up: fear took hold of me. I watched my father and the hand which was rubbing his face, unconsciously. At last he put the receiver down gently and turned towards me.

'She's had an accident,' he said. 'On the Esterel road. It took them a long time to find her address! They phoned Paris where they were given this number.'

He was speaking mechanically, with the same intonation, and I dared not interrupt him. 'The accident happened at the most dangerous place. It seems there have been a lot at this spot. The car fell 50 metres. it would have been a miracle if she had come out alive.'

C **1** rentra, **2** demanda, **3** été acheté, **4** coucha, **5** éveilla, **6** coupa, **7** demanda, **8** servait, **9** s'informa, **10** as commencé. **D** Marcel told his family that when he went into the room he could see the people were well-off, because they had furniture that looked like furniture in a museum, a piano and a large carpet in the dining room. He also told his family that the people had a large cupboard called a *livigroub*. Everyone was puzzled by this until his mother suggested it might be an English word. Joseph solved the mystery by realising that it was a living-room, in fact not the cupboard but the room where the cupboard was. Uncle Jules was disappointed by this, as he thought the word *livigroub* was rather poetic. **E À l'hippodrome:** 13, 19, 16, 18, 4, 21, 7, 2, 11, 15, 3. **En week-end:** 5, 9, 12, 1, 8, 14, 20, 10, 17, 6.

écoutez bien!   The deserter says he is not on earth to kill people. Wars are stupid and the world has had enough of them. He has seen fathers die, brothers go away and children cry. Mothers have suffered while others have a life of ease, despite the mud and blood. Some prisoners have been robbed of their soul, their wives and their past.

Faites le point! (unités 16–18)

1 (*Suggested answer*) Monsieur, Votre hôtel m'a été recommandé par des amis, les Pritchard, qui y ont passé leurs vacances il y a deux ans. Je vous serais reconnaissante de me donner vos prix de pension complète pour ma famille, c'est-à-dire mon mari, moi-même et nos deux filles âgées de 11 et 14 ans. Il nous faut deux chambres avec salle de bains ou douche. Je voudrais aussi savoir si l'hôtel est loin de la gare, car nous arriverons par le train. Nous aimerions rester à Cannes pendant les trois dernières semaines de juillet. Dans l'attente d'une prompte réponse, veuillez agréer, monsieur, l'expression de mes sentiments distingués. **2** 1f, 2e, 3a, 4h, 5d, 6g, 7c, 8b. **3 a** La voiture et les transports:

camion, capot, chariot, charrette, essence, pare-brise, pneu. **b** Les sports et les loisirs: chasse, fusil, baladeur, luge, patinoire, pêche, roman, télésiège, traîneau. **c** La santé et le corps humain: aveugle, boiter, cicatrice, consultation, muet, ordonnance, piqûre, torticolis. **4** 1e, 2b, 3h, 4d, 5g, 6a, 7f, 8c. **5** **a** aille, **b** vient, **c** soit, **d** fasse, **e** prend, **f** fait, **g** soit, **h** vienne. **6** 1c, 2e, 3d, 4a, 5f, 6b. **7** **a** Il faut que j'aille tout droit. **b** Il faut que je prenne la deuxième rue à gauche. **c** Il faut que je sois prudent. **d** Il ne faut pas que je boive d'alcool. **e** Il ne faut pas que je dépasse dans le virage. **f** Il faut que je respecte la limite de vitesse. **g** Il faut que j'aie de la patience. **h** Il faut que je fasse attention. **8** **a** ouvrit, **b** enleva, **c** jeta, **d** frappa, **e** répondit, **f** dit, **g** remercia, **h** se demanda.

Écoutez bien! – recording transcripts

Première unité

Femme	Bonjour, monsieur.
Fonctionnaire	Asseyez-vous! … Dossier 6529 … Voyons … Âge … Vous avez 40 ans.
Femme	C'est exact.
Fonctionnaire	Euh … Situation de famille … vous êtes célibataire.
Femme	Non, je suis mariée.
Fonctionnaire	Mais enfin, madame, c'est écrit ici, noir sur blanc, cé-li-ba-tai-re!
Femme	Je suis désolée, monsieur, mais je suis mariée depuis 15 ans!
Fonctionnaire	Vous êtes sûre?
Femme	Sûre et certaine! J'ai même trois enfants, deux filles et un garçon. Ils s'appellent …
Fonctionnaire	Comme vous voulez! Alors, mariée, trois enfants … Vous avez les yeux bleus …
Femme	Bruns. J'ai les yeux bruns.
Fonctionnaire	Bruns … et vous mesurez 1 m 50.
Femme	Mais enfin, regardez-moi, monsieur! Je mesure 1 m 80!
Fonctionnaire	Asseyez-vous, madame, je vous en prie … Alors … Profession … Archi…
Femme	Je suis dentiste.
Fonctionnaire	Merci. Passe-temps … Vous faites de la voile …
Femme	C'est vrai!

Fonctionnaire	Et vous jouez au bridge.
Femme	Ah non, je déteste jouer aux cartes. Mais, j'adore jouer aux échecs.
Fonctionnaire	Ah là là! É-checs … Bien … Adresse … Alors, je suppose que vous n'habitez pas 64, rue de Nancy, dans le 10ème arrondissement à Paris?
Femme	Correct! J'habite 178, avenue de New York, dans le 16ème.
Fonctionnaire	Donc, vous n'êtes pas Patricia Legros.
Femme	Non, je m'appelle Legris, Monique Legris, L-E-G-R-I-S.
Fonctionnaire	Et votre dossier est le numéro 6528, pas le numéro 6529!
Femme	Élémentaire, mon cher Watson!
Fonctionnaire	Euh … Non, je ne m'appelle pas Watson, je suis monsieur …

Deuxième unité

1	**Interviewer**	Pardon, jeune homme, je fais une enquête. Est-ce que je peux vous poser une question?
	Jeune homme	Si vous voulez.
	Interviewer	Avez-vous fait quelque chose d'intéressant samedi soir?
	Jeune homme	Je suis allé à la discothèque, avec ma sœur. J'ai beaucoup dansé. La musique était super! Nous y sommes restés très tard et j'ai été au lit à deux heures du matin.

2 **Interviewer** Pardon, madame. Je peux vous poser une question?

Femme Pas trop indiscrète, j'espère!

Interviewer Non! C'est pour une enquête. Je voudrais savoir si vous avez fait quelque chose d'intéressant samedi soir.

Femme Eh bien, j'ai pris un bain, j'ai mis une robe élégante et je suis allée au restaurant avec mon petit ami.

3 **Interviewer** Pardon, madame. Vous avez fait quelque chose d'intéressant samedi soir?

Femme Samedi dernier? J'ai une amie qui habite en Espagne depuis six mois. Je lui ai téléphoné.

Interviewer Vous avez bavardé longtemps?

Femme Oh, nous avons parlé environ une demi-heure, je pense.

4 **Interviewer** Avez-vous fait quelque chose d'intéressant samedi soir, monsieur?

Homme Samedi soir? Non, je n'ai rien fait de spécial. Je suis resté à la maison. J'ai allumé la télé vers neuf heures et j'ai regardé un film américain. Après ça, j'ai changé de chaîne pour voir une émission sur l'Angleterre.

5 **Interviewer** Excusez-moi, monsieur. Est-ce que vous avez fait quelque chose d'intéressant samedi soir?

Homme Je ne suis pas prêt d'oublier samedi soir! J'ai eu de la chance! Imaginez-vous que j'ai trouvé un billet de 50 euros, dans la rue! Alors, je suis allé au casino.

| **Interviewer** | Vous avez gagné quelque chose? |
| **Homme** | J'ai gagné 1000 euros, mais plus tard, j'en ai perdu 600! |

6	**Interviewer**	Pardon, mademoiselle …
	Jeune Femme	Madame! Je suis mariée.
	Interviewer	Pardon! Est-ce que vous avez fait quelque chose d'intéressant samedi soir?
	Jeune Femme	Non! Nous avons dîné chez mes beaux-parents. Nous avons parlé politique et, naturellement, nous nous sommes disputés, comme d'habitude!

Troisième unité

– Allô! … Salut, c'est Valentine! … Oui, ça va, ça va. Et vous? …L'hôtel? Il est dans un quartier très vieux, très pittoresque … Le problème, c'est que la plomberie laisse à désirer et qu'il n'y a jamais d'eau chaude … Oui, on mange bien ici, les spécialités régionales sont délicieuses … Il y a des tas de petits restaurants sympa et pas trop chers … J'ai grossi! J'ai déjà pris deux kilos! … Oui, il fait beau, il fait même très chaud. J'ai attrapé un coup de soleil … La plage est magnifique … La mer est bonne, mais on m'a dit qu'il y avait des requins! … Oui, il y a plein de choses à voir. Il y a des endroits très intéressants à visiter … Un château, un musée, un parc naturel … Mais il y a beaucoup de touristes … Les magasins de souvenirs sont super … il y a des choses vraiment originales … Bien sûr que je vous ai acheté des cadeaux, mais ça coûte très cher et je n'ai plus d'argent … Alors, au revoir, à bientôt! Moi aussi. Grosses bises à tout le monde!

Quatrième unité

Première partie: la télérecette d'aujourd'hui: la mousse au chocolat

Ingrédients: Quatre œufs, cent grammes de sucre en poudre, un demi verre de crème fraîche, cent cinquante grammes de chocolat noir en tablette. *Marche à suivre*: On fait fondre le chocolat dans deux ou trois cuillerées de café très fort. On casse les œufs, et on sépare les jaunes et les blancs. On incorpore les jaunes, le sucre, le chocolat et la crème fraîche. On ajoute les blancs d'œufs battus en neige très ferme. On met le dessert au frigidaire plusieurs heures avant de servir.

Deuxième partie: au restaurant

Cliente	S'il vous plaît, monsieur!
Serveur	Bonjour, madame. Vous avez choisi?
Cliente	Sur le menu à 18 euros, la soupe 'Maison', qu'est-ce que c'est?
Serveur	Aujourd'hui c'est de la soupe aux champignons, madame.
Cliente	Et le plat du jour, qu'est-ce que c'est?
Serveur	Du rôti de porc avec de la ratatouille.
Cliente	Et le dessert?
Serveur	Il reste seulement des pâtisseries, babas au rhum, mille-feuilles, éclairs…
Cliente	Et, dites-moi, la cuvée du chef, qu'est-ce que c'est?
Serveur	C'est un petit rosé de la région. Alors, vous prenez le menu à 18 euros, madame?
Cliente	Je suis désolée, mais c'est impossible!
Serveur	Impossible?
Cliente	Eh bien oui. J'ai peur de manger des champignons. C'est risqué, non? Je ne peux pas manger de viande parce que je

suis végétarienne, je ne peux pas manger de gâteaux parce que je suis au régime, et je n'aime pas le rosé.

Serveur   Et la ratatouille, madame?

Cliente   J'adore ça, mais 18 euros pour une ratatouille, vous plaisantez!

Cinquième unité

Première partie: dans une grande surface

1 Profitez de l'offre exceptionnelle de notre rayon 'jardin'. 20% de réduction sur tous les meubles de jardin. **2** Chers clients, aujourd'hui les camemberts sont en promotion à notre rayon crémerie. **3** Le petit Michel attend ses parents au bureau de renseignements qui est situé près de la sortie. **4** Du 1er au 15 juin, pour fêter le deuxième anniversaire de notre magasin, profitez de nos prix fous au rayon 'sport': Cinq T-shirts pour le prix de trois. **5** Notre magasin ferme dans dix minutes. Vous êtes priés de vous diriger vers les caisses de sortie.

Deuxième partie: dans la rue

1   – Je cherche un supermarché.

– Tournez à droite. Le supermarché est tout de suite à gauche.

2   – Vous connaissez un bon restaurant dans le quartier?

– Il y en a un excellent au-dessus du supermarché.

3   – Pardon, monsieur. La gare SNCF est loin d'ici?

– Non, elle est au bout de la rue.

4   – Où est la poste, s'il vous plaît?

– En face du marchand de fruits et légumes.

5   – Où se trouve la boucherie?

– Elle est entre le marchand de fruits et légumes et la pharmacie.

6 – Est-ce qu'il y a un bus pour aller à la piscine?

– Oui, prenez le 75. L'arrêt est devant la banque.

7 – Il y a un tabac par ici?

– Oui, il y a un débit de tabac au café là, vous voyez, à côté de l'Hôtel du Centre.

8 – J'ai besoin de pain et je voudrais acheter un gâteau pour le dessert.

– Il y a une boulangerie-pâtisserie entre le café-tabac et la crémerie.

Sixième unité

Section A

Jacques Pouvez-vous nous raconter exactement ce que vous avez fait et vu en une semaine en Corse.

Marlène Eh bien, j'ai pris l'avion de Paris à Ajaccio où j'ai tout de suite loué une voiture.

Jacques Qu'est-ce que vous avez fait à Ajaccio?

Marlène J'ai flâné sur le port, j'ai visité la vieille ville où il y a deux édifices à ne pas manquer, la cathédrale et la maison Bonaparte. On peut aussi visiter l'hôtel de ville où se trouve le musée napoléonien.

Jacques Quelle direction avez-vous prise après Ajaccio?

Marlène Je suis remontée vers le nord. J'ai longé la côte jusqu'au golfe de Porto. À Porto, il y a des falaises extraordinaires. Puis j'ai continué jusqu'à Evisa.

Jacques Qu'est-ce qu'on peut faire à Evisa?

Marlène Evisa a une situation idéale, à vingt-quatre kilomètres de la côte et à huit cent mètres d'altitude. On peut pêcher, faire de l'alpinisme et des promenades.

Jacques   Êtes-vous restée en montagne?

Marlène   Non, le lendemain je suis repassée par Porto, en route
pour Calvi. J'ai passé la journée sur la plage. On dit que
Calvi ne se visite pas, mais se regarde, car elle est d'une
beauté parfaite, mais on peut quand même faire le tour de
la forteresse.

Section B

Jacques   Vous êtes allée à Bastia?

Marlène   Oui, bien sûr. Je suis passée par l'Île-Rousse et par Saint-
Florent qui se trouve au fond d'un golfe majestueux. C'est
une station idéale pour les sports nautiques et c'est un
point de départ d'excursions à pied, en voiture ou en
bateau. À Bastia, il faut visiter la citadelle et aller prendre
un verre dans un des petits bars du vieux port. Il y a des
musées, des églises, mais il faut surtout regarder les gens
vivre! Le lendemain, j'ai pris la direction de la montagne.

Jacques   Vous êtes allée jusqu'à Corte?

Marlène   Non, arrivée à Morosaglia j'ai pris la route d'Asco où on
peut faire du ski en hiver. Le lendemain, j'ai pris la direction
de Cervione.

Jacques   C'est intéressant Cervione?

Marlène   La cathédrale vaut la peine d'être visitée. Ensuite, je suis
descendue jusqu'à Aléria où il y a des ruines grecques et
romaines, et les amateurs d'archéologie peuvent y visiter le
musée aménagé dans le vieux fort.

Section C

Jacques Vous êtes restée sur la côte?

Marlène Non, j'adore la montagne et je suis repartie en montagne! Je ne suis pas allée à Porto-Vecchio qui est une grande station balnéaire, ni à Bonifacio que je connais déjà très bien, mais sa situation est exceptionnelle, et il faut aller voir sa citadelle …

Jacques Il y a beaucoup de citadelles, forts, forteresses, etc., en Corse!

Marlène Oui, comme je l'ai mentionné plus tôt, c'est une île qui a connu de nombreuses invasions.

Jacques Mais revenons à votre voyage …

Marlène Oui, je voulais voir les mégalithes du plateau de Cauria. C'est un des grands sites de la recherche préhistorique, il y a des dolmens et des menhirs extraordinaires dispersés dans la nature. J'ai passé la nuit à Sartène.

Jacques Et votre tour de Corse tire à sa fin?

Marlène Hélas, oui! Il me reste la dernière étape que j'ai faite en longeant la côte, de Sartène à Ajaccio, en passant par Propriano qui est une des plus belles stations balnéaires de la Méditerranée.

Jacques C'est tout dire!

Huitième unité

Fille J'aime bien l'école. Mes matières préférées sont les maths et les sciences. Je voudrais faire des études supérieures pour avoir un bon métier. Je m'intéresse beaucoup aux maladies et j'aime bien le contact avec les gens. J'ai besoin d'un travail intéressant, varié et bien payé parce que j'adore dépenser de l'argent!

Garçon Je déteste l'école et je n'ai pas l'intention de faire des études. Je veux faire un métier manuel. J'adore les voitures et les motos. Mon frère vient d'acheter une moto d'occasion et je l'aide à la réparer. C'est génial! Mon ambition, c'est d'avoir un petit garage et de travailler à mon compte.

Fille Moi, je voudrais voir le monde, découvrir des pays complètement différents du mien. J'adore voyager. J'aime bien rencontrer toutes sortes de gens différents et bavarder avec eux. Je parle couramment l'anglais et je me débrouille en espagnol. J'aime bien le travail en équipe et j'adore les hommes en uniforme!

Garçon Je déteste la campagne. C'est ennuyeux, c'est beaucoup trop calme pour mon goût. J'ai besoin du bruit et de l'activité des grandes villes, surtout le soir. Et je déteste la routine. J'aime l'idée que chaque jour va être différent. J'adore conduire et je viens de m'acheter une voiture. Je connais la ville comme ma poche: les endroits touristiques, les boîtes de nuit, les bons restaurants, les théâtres, les cinémas.

Neuvième unité

'Allô Suzanne? … C'est Françoise! … Oui, ça va très bien, et toi? … Toute la famille va bien. Claude et Liliane viennent enfin de décider où ils iront en vacances cet été … En Bretagne … Non. Ils ne loueront pas de villa parce qu'ils ne veulent pas rester au même endroit … À l'hôtel? Oh non, c'est trop cher! Ils feront du camping … Ils iront à la plage, ils se baigneront, ils prendront des bains de soleil … Les enfants joueront aux boules et au ballon sur la plage … Bien sûr qu'ils feront du sport! Les garçons feront de la voile … Non, Colette a peur, mais elle jouera au tennis et elle essaiera de faire du cheval … Oui, Claude ira à la pêche, il a déjà acheté tout le matériel! … Ils iront au restaurant, je crois qu'ils mangeront beaucoup de poissons et de crustacés … Ils iront aussi dans les crêperies, naturellement, les enfants adorent les crêpes … Claude goûtera sûrement au cidre breton mais je suis certaine qu'il préférera le nôtre! … Oui, ils verront probablement des calvaires, des dolmens et des menhirs, il y en a presque partout … Colette espère bien voir une fête folklorique, surtout pour les costumes et les coiffes de dentelles. Malheureusement Liliane a horreur du biniou!'

Dixième unité

Première partie: la météo

Et voici Marcel Brel avec le bulletin spécial météo-vacances. «Chers auditeurs, bonjour! Et bonjour en particulier aux estivants qui se préparent à partir en vacances aujourd'hui. Malheureusement, vous n'avez pas de chance au point de vue météo. Eh oui, comme vous l'avez déjà deviné, il y aura des averses un peu partout, même dans le Midi, et elles seront particulièrement fortes en Bretagne. Il y aura aussi quelques chutes de neige en montagne, mais rassurez-vous, seulement au-dessus de 2000 mètres. Vent de secteur nord-nord-ouest, donc il fera très frais le long de la côte normande. Si vous partez en fin de semaine, vous aurez plus de chance. Le temps s'améliorera à partir de jeudi. Il y aura des éclaircies sur la côte atlantique et du soleil dans le Midi. Aujourd'hui, les températures minimales seront comprises entre 6 et 10 degrés. Les maximums atteindront 12 à 16 degrés sur la moitié nord, 16 à 19 degrés sur la moitié sud du pays. Au revoir, et bonnes vacances!»

Deuxième partie: les vacances

Enquêteur	Pardon madame, vous avez déjà fait vos projets de vacances?
Femme	Oui, nous avons décidé de passer nos vacances en Normandie cette année. Nous descendrons dans un petit hôtel à Caen et nous y resterons huit jours.
Enquêteur	Pourquoi la Normandie?
Femme	Eh bien, je suis d'origine normande!
Enquêteur	Eh que ferez-vous quand vous serez en Normandie?
Femme	Nous aimons beaucoup visiter les villes historiques avec des maisons typiques, de vieux bâtiments, alors nous verrons probablement les deux abbayes à Caen, par exemple.
Enquêteur	Irez-vous à Bayeux?
Femme	Pour voir la fameuse tapisserie de la reine Mathilde? Sans aucun doute!
Enquêteur	Mademoiselle, s'il vous plaît?
Jeune Fille	Monsieur?
Enquêteur	Si cela ne vous dérange pas, j'aimerais vous poser quelques questions à propos de vos vacances.
Jeune Fille	Mes vacances?

Enquêteur	Oui, vous partirez bien en vacances cet été?
Jeune Fille	Ah oui, c'est déjà décidé, j'irai en Corse.
Enquêteur	Pourquoi la Corse?
Jeune Fille	L'idée me plaît c'est tout, et en plus j'adore la mer et le soleil.
Enquêteur	Et que ferez-vous là-bas?
Jeune Fille	Je me baignerai, je ferai de la plongée sous-marine, de la voile, je ferai des randonnées à cheval …
Enquêteur	Vous êtes donc sportive?
Jeune Fille	Oui, j'adore le sport.
Enquêteur	Et dites-moi, descendrez-vous dans un hôtel?
Jeune Fille	Absolument pas! Je ferai du camping ou bien je dormirai en plein air sur la plage!
Enquêteur	Et vous passerez combien de temps en Corse?
Jeune Fille	Oh, je ne sais pas exactement, cinq ou six semaines.
Enquêteur	Monsieur, permettez-moi de vous poser quelques questions à propos de vos vacances.
Homme	Avec plaisir! Allez-y monsieur!
Enquêteur	Vous avez déjà fait des projets?
Homme	Ah oui bien sûr, je resterai ici.
Enquêteur	Comment!
Homme	Je resterai ici, comme d'habitude.
Enquêteur	Vous passerez vos vacances chez vous?
Homme	Oui c'est ça.
Enquêteur	Et vous ne vous ennuierez pas?
Homme	Ah non pas du tout!
Enquêteur	Que ferez-vous donc?

Homme	Je me lèverai tard, je lirai le journal en fumant la pipe, j'irai au petit café du coin et j'y passerai toute la journée à boire, à jouer aux cartes et à bavarder avec des amis.
Enquêteur	Combien de temps serez-vous en vacances?
Homme	Un mois. Fin août ce sera fini, malheureusement.
Enquêteur	Comment ça?
Homme	Le 31 août, ma femme rentrera à la maison!

Onzième unité

Allô. Je voudrais voir votre chef des ventes. Je serai à Paris les 11 et 12 mai. Est-ce que je peux passer dans vos bureaux à ce moment-là? Je suis Monsieur Lapoix, L-A-P-O-I-X. Mon téléphone est le 02.51.16.35.67 et mon e-mail: lapoix@aol.com. **Mardi, 13h48.** Bonjour. Mademoiselle Duval à l'appareil. Je suis la secrétaire de Madame Dumas, D-U-M-A-S. J'ai un message de sa part pour votre directeur. Madame Dumas s'excuse mais elle a dû changer la date de sa visite à Paris. Elle arrivera le 18 avril, et non le 16 comme prévu. **Mardi, 14h05.** Allô! Ici monsieur Tanguy, T-A-N-G-U-Y, de la société Meublot et Fils. Nous vous avons demandé un catalogue il y a environ un mois et nous ne l'avons toujours pas reçu. Pourriez-vous nous en faire parvenir un autre, de toute urgence, à l'adresse suivante: Société Meublot et Fils: Meublot, M-E-U-B-L-O-T, 72 boulevard de la Résistance, 28005, Chartres. Merci d'avance. **Mardi, 14h17.** Ici Madame Aubry, A-U-B-R-Y. Je voudrais des précisions sur un des articles de votre catalogue. Il s'agit du numéro HK628. Pourriez-vous me rappeler au 02.96.58.15.44 le plus tôt possible. Merci. **Mardi, 14h36.**

Douzième unité

À la plage

1 Le temps était couvert. Il y avait beaucoup de nuages dans le ciel.
2 Un petit garçon et une petite fille jouaient au ballon. **3** Un petit garçon faisait un château de sable avec son père. **4** Deux jeunes femmes, couchées sur le dos, prenaient un bain de soleil. **5** Un jeune garçon nageait le crawl. **6** Un couple de personnes âgées dormait, assis sur des chaises longues. **7** Ils avaient les pieds dans l'eau. **8** Ils portaient des lunettes noires pour se protéger du soleil. **9** Une petite fille ramassait des coquillages. **10** D'autres enfants pêchaient. **11** Une jeune femme vendait des glaces. **12** Trois enfants mangeaient une glace.

Treizième unité

Comparaison entre la Guyane française et Madagascar:

	LA GUYANE FRANÇAISE	MADAGASCAR
Superficie	91 000 km²	587 000 km²
Altitude maximum	Montagne Tabulaire: 830 m	Amboro: 2876 m
Latitude	5 degrés Nord	20 degrés Sud
Longitude	53 degrés Ouest	45 degrés Est

Quatorzième unité

Première partie

Homme Assistance Prima. Qu'y a-t-il pour votre service?

Femme Allô! Bonsoir, monsieur. J'espère que vous allez pouvoir me venir en aide le plus vite possible. Ma voiture est tombée en panne dans la forêt et je suis toute seule!

Homme Ne vous inquiétez, madame, nous somme là pour ça. Où êtes-vous exactement?

Femme Quelque part sur la nationale 12, entre Rennes et Fougères.

Homme Et vous rouliez dans quel sens?

Femme Je venais de Rennes.

Homme Et vous êtes partie quand?

Femme J'ai quitté la maison ce soir vers huit heures.

Homme Alors, il est maintenant 20 heures 15, donc vous ne devez pas être très loin de Rennes. Quel est votre numéro d'adhésion?

Femme Attendez… Voyons… Ah, voilà! C'est le GH 52.33.86.

Homme Et votre numéro d'immatriculation?

Femme 567 IMP 35.

Homme Et la marque, le modèle et la couleur du véhicule?

Femme C'est une Peugeot 206 rouge.

Homme Attendez un instant, je vous prie … Alors, vous êtes bien Madame Dupont, D-U-P-O-N-T, Madame Claude Dupont?

Femme C'est exact.

Homme La dépanneuse sera avec vous dans environ trois quarts d'heure.

Femme   Dans trois quarts d'heure! C'est bien long et l'endroit où je suis est très isolé.

Homme   Nous ferons de notre mieux pour arriver le plus tôt possible, madame.

Troisième partie

Femme   Qu'y a-t-il pour votre service, monsieur?

Homme   Je voudrais changer le pull que j'ai acheté dans ce magasin. Il a rétréci.

Femme   Faites voir, monsieur. Hmm! Vous avez bien suivi les instructions de lavage?

Homme   Moi, non. Mais ma femme fait toujours très attention à ce genre de choses. J'ai porté le pull une fois, puis elle l'a lavé et elle l'a rangé. Quand je l'ai mis hier j'ai remarqué qu'il avait rétréci.

Femme   Vous faites quelle taille, monsieur?

Homme   Je ne sais pas exactement. Je vois quelque chose qui me plaît et je l'essaye. Je ne regarde pas les étiquettes!

Femme   Mmm. Vous n'avez pas grossi par hasard?

Homme   Certainement pas! Ma femme me fait faire un régime très sévère à cause de mon cholestérol!

Femme   En général on ne fait pas de remboursement. Mais exceptionnellement …

Homme   Je préférerais le changer. J'ai le reçu, tenez. Vous me rendrez un grand service… En plus, ma femme n'aime pas tellement cette couleur … Vous ne l'avez pas en marron, je suppose?

Quinzième unité

Première partie

– Allô. Tropical Hôtel, bonjour!

– Bonjour, monsieur. Pourriez-vous me donner quelques renseignements sur votre hôtel?

– Avec plaisir, madame.

– Nous passons quelques jours à Avignon et je cherche un hôtel qui se trouve dans un quartier calme.

– Le Tropical est à dix minutes du centre-ville, madame, mais il est entouré de grands jardins où il y a des tennis, une piscine couverte avec sauna et un mini-golf.

– C'est formidable. Mais mon mari est handicapé et supporte mal la chaleur.

– Ne vous inquiétez pas, madame. Nous avons plusieurs ascenseurs, toutes nos chambres sont climatisées et en plus, l'hôtel est aménagé pour handicapés.

– Et en ce qui concerne la restauration?

– Alors, nous avons trois restaurants, dont un self-service, et deux bars, dont un en terrasse.

– Excellent! Y a-t-il des offres spéciales pour les retraités?

– Ah non, madame, je suis désolé, nous faisons seulement des réductions pour les enfants de moins de douze ans.

– Tant pis. Une dernière question. J'ai un adorable petit caniche blanc…

– Je regrette, madame, nous n'acceptons pas les chiens, même dans les chambres!

Deuxième partie

1 – Pardon madame, j'ai besoin d'une pièce pour le chariot. Je n'ai pas de monnaie.

– Allez à la caisse au supermarché et on changera votre billet.

2 – Pardon madame, il n'y a pas de serviettes dans la salle de bains.

– Je suis désolée, monsieur. La femme de chambre va vous en apporter tout de suite.

– Et le lit n'est pas fait.

– Je vais lui demander de changer les draps en même temps.

3 – Bonjour monsieur, je voudrais changer la robe que j'ai achetée dans votre magasin. Je l'ai lavée une fois et elle a rétréci.

– Vous avez le reçu? Très bien … Je suis désolé, mais je n'ai plus votre taille. Voulez-vous voir un autre modèle ou préférez-vous être remboursée?

– Je préfère être remboursée.

4 – Mademoiselle, s'il vous plaît!

– Monsieur?

– La viande est dure, le pain est rassis et en plus, j'ai une fourchette sale. Je voudrais parler au patron.

– Je suis désolée monsieur, mais c'est son jour de congé!

5 – Bonjour monsieur. Pourriez-vous me dépanner le plus vite possible. J'ai une fuite d'eau dans la cuisine et c'est une véritable inondation!

– Je suis désolé, le plombier est pris toute la journée aujourd'hui. Si vous voulez, je peux vous donner un autre numéro qui fonctionne 24 heures sur 24.

Seizième unité

Dialogue 1

Homme Si on te téléphonait en pleine nuit, disons à 2 ou 3 heures du matin, comment réagirais-tu?

Femme D'abord, je serais très inquiète, naturellement. Je me demanderais si quelqu'un a eu un accident. Mais si c'était une mauvaise plaisanterie ou même une erreur, je crois que je serais furieuse!

Dialogue 2

Femme 1 Tu regardes souvent des vidéos?

Femme 2 Oui, j'adore!

Femme 1 Si tu louais une vidéo pour la soirée, une histoire d'amour tragique, comme *West Side Story* par exemple, qu'est-ce que tu ferais?

Femme 2 Je m'installerais confortablement devant la télé avec une énorme boîte de mouchoirs en papier.

Femme 1 Pourquoi?

Femme 2 Parce que je sais que c'est une histoire qui finit mal et que je pleurerais. Je suis très sentimentale.

Dialogue 3

Femme Si tu étais dans un grand magasin ou un supermarché et si la caissière te rendait trop de monnaie, que ferais-tu?

Homme Si j'étais très pauvre, je ne dirais peut-être rien, mais comme en ce moment je gagne bien ma vie, je le dirais à la caissière parce que sinon, c'est elle qui aurait des ennuis!

Dialogue 4

Femme Si vous gagniez beaucoup beaucoup d'argent, une somme énorme, comme le gros lot à la Loterie Nationale ou au Loto, qu'est-ce que vous feriez?

Homme Ah, le rêve, mais j'aurais du mal à y croire! D'abord, j'en investirais une partie, puis j'arrêterais de travailler et je voyagerais. Et pour la première fois de ma vie, je dépenserais sans compter. Je ferais aussi plein de cadeaux à ma famille et à mes amis et je donnerais de l'argent à des associations caritatives et pour la recherche médicale. Mais ça m'étonnerait beaucoup de gagner, parce que je n'achète jamais de billet de loterie!

Dix-septième unité

À Saint Maurice la consultation gratuite commence. Voici la dame en noir, solide paysanne de 45 ans. Knock l'examine et lui apprend qu'elle a dû, étant petite, tomber d'une grande échelle de 3 m 50.

Knock (*la fait asseoir*) Vous vous rendez compte de votre état?

La dame Non.

Knock (*il s'assied en face d'elle*) Tant mieux. Vous avez envie de guérir, ou vous n'avez pas envie?

La dame J'ai envie.

Knock J'aime mieux vous prévenir tout de suite que ce sera très long et très coûteux.

La dame Ah! mon Dieu! Et pourquoi ça?

Knock Parce qu'on ne guérit pas en cinq minutes un mal qu'on traîne depuis 40 ans.

La dame   Depuis 40 ans?

Knock   Oui, depuis que vous êtes tombée de votre échelle.

La dame   Et combien est-ce que ça me coûterait?

Knock   Qu'est-ce que valent les veaux, actuellement?

La dame   Ça dépend du marché et de la grosseur. Mais on ne peut guère en avoir de propres à moins de quatre ou cinq cents francs.

Knock   Et les cochons gras?

La dame   Il y en a qui font plus de mille.

Knock   Eh bien! ça vous coûtera à peu près deux cochons et deux veaux.

La dame   Ah! là là! Près de trois mille francs? C'est une désolation, Jésus, Marie!

Knock   Si vous aimez mieux faire un pèlerinage, je ne vous en empêche pas.

La dame   Oh! un pèlerinage, ça revient cher aussi et ça ne réussit pas souvent. (*un silence*) Mais qu'est-ce que je peux donc avoir de si terrible que ça?

Knock   (*avec une grande courtoisie*) Je vais vous l'expliquer en une minute au tableau noir. (*il va au tableau et commence un croquis*) Voici votre moelle épinière, en coupe, très schématiquement, n'est-ce pas? Vous reconnaissez ici votre faisceau de Turck et ici votre colonne de Clarke. Vous me suivez? Eh bien! quand vous êtes tombée de l'échelle, votre Turck et votre Clarke ont glissé en sens inverse (*il trace des flèches*) de quelques dixièmes de millimètres. Vous me direz que c'est très peu.